WRITERS AND THEIR WORK

ISOBEL ARMSTRONG
General Editor

BRYAN LOUGHREY
Advisory Editor

Julius Caesar

Death of Caesar

This image invites readers to compare the treachery that Caesar
encounters with the attacks that Portia makes on her own body.
Probably the earliest visual account of Caesar's murder to be circulated
widely in Europe, this woodcut illustrates the 1473 edition of
Boccaccio's *Lives of Famous Women.*

WW

William Shakespeare

Julius Caesar

Mary Hamer

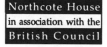
Northcote House
in association with the
British Council

Front cover illustration   **Bust of Julius Caesar**

This idealized portrait head of Julius Caesar was made more than twenty years after his death under the rule of Octavian/Augustus, who wished to exploit the image of Caesar for his own political ends.

© Copyright 1998 by Mary Hamer

First published in 1998 by Northcote House Publishers Ltd, Plymbridge House, Estover Road, Plymouth PL6 7PY, United Kingdom.
Tel: +44 (01752) 202368 Fax: +44 (01752) 202330.

British Library Cataloguing-in-Publication Data
A catalogue record for this book is available from the British Library

ISBN 0-7463-0871-X

Typeset by PDQ Typesetting, Newcastle-under-Lyme
Printed and bound in the United Kingdom

For my stepson, Daniel,
and
in happy memory of my father, Laurence Turner

Contents

Illustrations

Acknowledgements

I should like to thank Harriet Lutzky, who first taught me to think about the connection between mothers and the sacred, and to express my gratitude to both Gilligans, Carol and Jim, for the help their work has given me in framing an understanding of the violence of Rome. It was under the auspices of Shakespeare & Company, as the student of Tina Packer and Dennis Krausnick, that I learned to connect Shakespeare's text with the body. Without that teaching and without the work of Normi Noel on the language of young boys, I should not have been able to make sense of this play. My thanks also to Alison Keith, who very generously read this work in draft.

Illustration Acknowledgements

The publishers and the author gratefully acknowledge the following for supplying illustrations and granting permission for their use. Acknowledgements are listed according to plate numbers.

Cover: Monumenti Musei e Gallerie Pontificie, Vatican City, Italy; *Frontispiece*: Department of Printing and Graphic Arts, The Houghton Library, Harvard University, Cambridge, USA; 1. *The Oxford Companion to Classical Literature* by Sir Paul Harvey, by permission of Oxford University Press, Oxford, UK; 2. POPPERFOTO/Reuters, photograph by Paolo Cocco; 3. By permission of the Syndics of Cambridge University Library, Cambridge, UK; 4. Stephen Warren Miles (Class of 1957) and Marilyn Ross Miles Foundation Purchase Fund. The Herbert F. Johnson Museum of Art, Cornell University, New York, USA; 5. N. A. Cumpsty; 6. The *Guardian*/M&G Group.

Abbreviations

Quotations from *Julius Caesar* are taken from the New Cambridge Shakespeare edition, edited by Marvin Spevack (Cambridge, 1988). All other Shakespeare quotations are taken from the *Riverside Shakespeare*, edited by G. Blakemore Evans (Boston, 1974).

FM   *The Female Malady: Women, Madness and English Culture 1830–1980*, by Elaine Showalter (London, 1987)

HWC   'Here Was a Caesar!', by Jasper Griffin, *New York Review of Books* (1988), vol. 35, no. 8, p. 14(4)

JC   *Julius Caesar* by William Shakespeare, edited by Marvin Spevack (Cambridge, 1988)

OCCL *Oxford Companion to Classical Literature*, edited by Paul Harvey (Oxford, 1980)

1

Where Fantasy and History Meet

> For, men striving who should most honour him, they made him hateful and troublesome to themselves that most favoured him, by reason of the unmeasurable greatness and honours which they gave him.
>
> (Plutarch, *The Life of Julius Caesar*, trans. Sir Thomas North (*JC* 155))

A dream of Caesar mingles with the world of Hamlet; it haunts his play as a second spectral presence, a shadow behind the dead father's more famous ghost. It is with Julius Caesar, or with a travesty of Caesar, that Shakespeare asks us to identify Polonius the Renaissance courtier and intellectual, the man whose name is so close to the classical one, Apollonius, that was borne by a grammarian long ago. Shakespeare makes Polonius volunteer that when he was at the university he had taken the part of Caesar in one of their dull Latin plays: 'I did enact Julius Caesar. /I was kill'd i' th' Capitol. Brutus kill'd me' (*Hamlet*, 3.2.103–4). This might perhaps suggest to us, as his audience, that along with the New Learning, notions about relationship and power, notions where intimacy was identified with betrayal, were passed on at the university to Hamlet the student as they had been to Polonius before. The figure of the murdered Caesar resonated in the imagination of Shakespeare even when he was not directly engaged in writing a Roman play. He may well have felt that the world in which he lived himself was a Roman one.

There's a special name, *'trahison des clercs'*, for the betrayal that is performed by intellectuals as a group. It's used to describe what happens when they compromise the pursuit of understanding and choose to become collaborators, to identify with the state. Shakespeare seems to have had reservations about the classical heritage and about what embracing it meant for the time in which he himself lived. In *Hamlet* the audience sees that same Polonius killed as he stands behind the arras in Gertrude's room. Could this be a modern example of intimacy betrayed? Brutus stabbed Caesar, the man who loved him: Hamlet claims not to know the man who is standing spying on him in his mother's room. Is there a link in Shakespeare's mind that we don't know of, a link that may surface also in his play of *Julius Caesar*, one that connects Rome and the death of Caesar with confusion, with ignorance in educated men and with trouble between mothers and sons?

In Plutarch, Shakespeare's chief source for *Julius Caesar*, 'hugger-mugger' is the word that Antony uses to fend off the suggestion that once murdered, Caesar should be buried in secrecy. When the conspirators would like to get his dead body out of the way, Antony objects that Caesar 'should be honourably buried and not in hugger-mugger'(*JC* 170). It is for the vernacular phrase 'hugger-mugger' that Shakespeare reaches when he makes Claudius reflect on the burial of Polonius. 'We have done but greenly/In hugger-mugger to inter him', Claudius admits, picking up the word just as the tradition of Rome had been picked up throughout Europe (*Hamlet*, 4.5.83–5). We were naïve to get rid of the body like that he says. A folly that involves disposing of bodies, as well as killing them, seems to be at stake for Shakespeare as he confronts the heritage of Rome. A mistake that will have its effects on daughters, perhaps too? Claudius completes the iambic pentameter, with the words 'Poor Ophelia'. He speaks of Ophelia in the same breath as her dead father. 'We have done but greenly/In hugger-mugger to inter him; poor Ophelia'. When Shakespeare brings the Roman tradition to mind his fantasy speaks of dead and shrouded bodies and of women, of mothers alienated from their sons and of daughters driven into madness by their distress.

These images arose almost incidentally when Shakespeare was engaged in telling a story about modern, or at least early modern times, the times in which he himself lived. We might ask ourselves today, as we approach the play of *Julius Caesar*, what it meant for Shakespeare to turn back and focus his full attention on Roman history and to offer his own account of

2

Caesar's death. Why should it matter to Shakespeare, why should it matter to us today, this story from the past?

True stories that come to us from the past are what we call history; if we keep them alive among ourselves it is in the hope that they may help to account for the conditions still shaping our own lives in the present. When Plutarch, a man writing in Greek, who was born north of Attica, was writing his lives of famous men in the second century, it was a way of explaining the political conditions of the world in which he and his contemporaries found themselves, a world that was governed from Rome by one man. The empire, that is the rule of Rome, extended round the Mediterranean, across North Africa from Egypt right round to Spain and reached beyond that to southern Britain (see plate 1).

In telling how famous individuals struggled for power, as Plutarch did, one sort of explanation for the creation of the Roman empire was implied. Plutarch chose to write what he called a set of *Parallel Lives*, comparing each Roman leader with a Greek one, perhaps to remind his readers that before Rome ruled the world it was Greeks who exercised authority round the Mediterranean. But an empire is not just an enormous extent of territory that has been annexed by military force and brought under alien rule, an empire is a form of government, a form that invests extraordinary power and authority in the figure of a single man. The story of the founding of the Roman empire, when it is told in terms of the life-history or the public career of one man, succeeds in disguising a crucial political question. It avoids asking whether there is a link between telling stories about heroes and creating a culture in which competition, competition between men, is silently made into an ideal in itself. There might be other models, you know, for human develop-ment and growth: doesn't the vernacular tradition of Europe, the voice that speaks through what we call folktales, often emphasize the importance of co-operation? Though Plutarch is apparently tracing the shift from one form of government to another, whether he is writing about the Roman republic or the Roman empire, in each case he is describing the struggle for power that takes place between men.

William Shakespeare, writing in English at the start of the

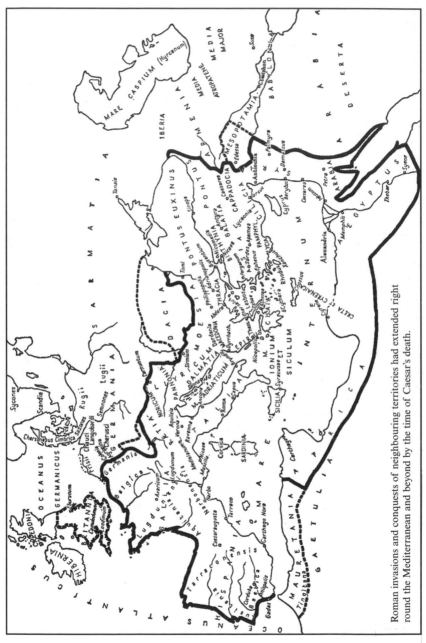

Roman invasions and conquests of neighbouring territories had extended right round the Mediterranean and beyond by the time of Caesar's death.

Plate 1 A map of the Roman Empire under Augustus

4

seventeenth century, like Plutarch had a use for the past. But Shakespeare was a poet rather than a historian. When he told stories it was in the form of plays and the effect of his work was to open up questions, questions about the world of the present, rather than to offer to explain it. Some questions, though, were not easy to ask in England at that time, even questions about what sort of man made a good king: Queen Elizabeth took exception to a private staging of Shakespeare's *Richard II* given at what she took to be the wrong moment. Questions about the very form of government, about whether having kings at all was a good idea, were not safe.

It was almost impossible to frame such questions for an audience in a world ruled by monarchs who, it was claimed, drew their authority direct from the Christian god. Accounts of the Great Chain of Being can make it sound charming, with its elaborate and detailed descent down through the orders of angels to man and beyond that through the beasts down to the very stones of the earth, but it would be a pity to miss the fact that this theology has a political force. It suggests that some human beings are more like god than others and it makes differences of status and of authority between them – between priest and people, between women and men, between poor men and rich men – seem natural. Isn't that what's known as mystification, when appeals to invisible abstractions are offered, instead of naming the desire for power and authority in human beings?

Stories from the Roman past presented Shakespeare with the opportunity that stories from the history of England could not provide. For the stories of Julius Caesar and of Antony and Cleopatra that he took from Plutarch allowed him to confront and to represent a world in which one political order was yielding to another and to remind his audience that there had once existed an alternative to the location of supreme power in one man. Rather than presenting monarchical authority as a given, like the laws of nature, as he does in *Henry V* or *Hamlet*, which were both written about this time, in *Julius Caesar* Shakespeare used drama to explore the desire that human beings have to be first, and to ask about the part played by that desire in shaping the forms of government set in place by men.

He was set free to reframe the connection between religion and politics at the same time, to ask questions about the stories that were told in the name of religion – stories which are sometimes known as myths – and about the religious practices or rituals that commemorated those myths and built them into the structure of everyday experience. In Shakespeare's England, Elizabeth, who had been on the throne since before the playwright himself had been born, chose to strengthen her own position as queen by deliberately associating herself with the cult of the Virgin Mary.[1] Even more telling had been the move she made on her accession, when she took control of all religious observance within her kingdom. She made it compulsory to follow the forms specified in the Prayer Book that she issued in 1559 and made attendance at church on Sunday obligatory. Her authority did not stop short at specifying readings from the Scriptures for different days of the year. Under the form of shaping Christian observance day by day, the Prayer Book was an attempt to use language and ritual to reach into her subjects' inner lives, in order as it were to provide them with a script. Private identities were to be standardized, as Foucault might have put it, by repeated and regular exposure to controlled events including readings from selected texts of scripture and the communion service. Elizabeth was an exceptional woman, for an accident of birth had given her a position of authority as monarch; one that was normally reserved for men. Shakespeare noted that Roman religion, as he found it described in Plutarch, seemed equally political in its effects and equally indisposed to favour women.

Julius Caesar was the first of the stories that Shakespeare took via Plutarch from Roman history and it begins when the Roman republic is still in place. When responsibility for protecting the life of the community in Rome was organized under the forms that were called the republic (*res publica*, affairs of state, business), authority was shared between different complementary offices of the state and men were elected to these offices for fixed terms. For men of the ruling classes in Rome, the patricians, this represented an advance in their personal dignity: this sharing out of power between them, taking turns, was the consequence of the decision to stop having kings. It is often said that when the last of the Tarquins, who had ruled as monarchs, was driven out of Rome it was in order to be rid of monarchy, since it so easily led to tyranny when power was

Mary Hauer

N $\quad 5^{2}$

NL

⊘ 5^{2} -

PRL $\quad 2^{5}$ - 5^{3} - 6

concentrated in a single pair of hands. But this explanation fails to register another constitutional change that was being made at that time. When Rome got rid of its kings it allowed a separation to be made between the religious and the judicial functions of the state. Under the republic, judicial power was divided between two consuls, in order to limit the authority of each one, while the man who held the office known as *Pontifex Maximus* acted as chief representative in religious matters of the ancient kings of Rome. As such he took responsibility for organized religious observance. It was, if you like, an early version of disestablishment, that formal separation of church and state that has often been proposed in Britain as an improvement and as a means to clearer political thought. More realistic attitudes too: today, as many people have argued, disestablishment might lead to a more humane treatment of the relationship between Mrs Parker Bowles and Prince Charles.

Yet Rome had not entirely made away with exceptional individual honours. A victorious general could apply to be granted a triumph if he had killed sufficient numbers of enemy troops, that is over 5,000 of them: a triumph meant that he was permitted to lead his troops and his captives through the city, while its inhabitants cheered. The supreme power of one individual man continued to be acknowledged in Rome even though it was no longer given political form in the authority of a single ruler, the monarch. It was represented instead through this staged public action, a bit like the return of a single sports hero today, the ritual in which honour was heaped on one man at his formal triumph. It's enough to make you think that masculinity itself was being worshipped, or at least a militarized form of it in Rome, a deformation of masculinity as some would say. The occasion offered a way of representing violence, a capacity for destruction that is present in all human beings, but of representing it as a masculine attribute. Through the formal organization of the triumph the horror of destruction was taken away. The man being honoured was always a military commander, responsible for the deaths of many other men. Julius Caesar himself, as it happens, claimed to have caused 1,192,000 deaths (*HWC* 14).

Shakespeare begins his play of *Julius Caesar* on the day when Caesar had been accorded a triumph: he seems to have agreed,

7

as a dramatist, that the military ritual of the triumph opens a window for us into the internal economy of Rome, into its religion and its civilization. It suggests that the cultural and political order which produced famous heroes like Caesar, who is celebrated as a great classical author as well as a military leader, created them at the cost of respect for the business of ordinary life and for the lives of other nameless men. (These too had a part to play at a triumph, whether they were subordinated in the ranks as soldiers, made to walk with bowed heads as captives or enlisted as anonymous spectators to give applause. The mangled bodies that had paid for the triumph, at least the enemy ones, were present in the form of statistics.) But Caesar, like other heroes, came to a violent end. As Shakespeare would discover, through the process of writing his play, a man living within reach of the civilization of Rome, whatever his status, might find himself inescapably at risk. Though they made up elaborate rules for their war games, Romans did not always observe them. The triumph that opens Shakespeare's play was awarded to the historical Caesar following the defeat not of foreigners but of Pompey, the man who was married to Julia, Caesar's own daughter.

When the Roman republic failed, as it is usually expressed, though it might be fairer to say that it was destroyed, it was followed by the empire: this meant that kings were restored again but under another name, one that had a military history. *Imperator* was originally the title by which troops hailed their general after a victory. (The general assumed the title after his name until the end of his magistracy or until his triumph. The constitutional changes, the sharing of power and the separation of religious from political authority that might have opened the way to fresh patterns of thought were lost.) Some people think of the republic as a noble experiment that did not survive because its time had not yet come but that sounds like using the figure of History as a secular version of the figure of god in accounting for human affairs. When Shakespeare based *Julius Caesar* on the events that had brought the Roman republic to an end, he was telling a story about the desire for power in men, men of the governing class, in a culture that had chosen to identify itself with military violence. Rome chose aggrandisement through conquest and domination as the means of creating authority for

8

itself in the human world. What about the way powerful Romans treated the nameless men inside Rome, Shakespeare asked, men like himself, who made up the crowd? He wondered, too, about relations between women and men under such a regime.

As an actor who himself wrote plays, Shakespeare may already have been struck by the absence of women's voices in the public debates and arguments of Rome, already have been wondering about what that implied. Why else, in his earlier work, *The Merchant of Venice*, did Shakespeare give the name of Portia, who was the wife of Brutus and the daughter of Cato, to a woman who spoke out in public but could only do so when she was disguised as a man? Portia raises her voice in court in order to speak of mercy. In *Julius Caesar* it is Shakespeare himself who asks about the law that brings down such harm on Roman men, or as we might say today, on men of the western tradition. Why do they sabotage the political system they have struggled to put into place? What makes them both want and not want to set up a king?

Today British readers at least live in the shadow of our own eighteenth century, sometimes known as the Augustan age, when the authority of classical civilization was re-endorsed. The first Roman to be called emperor received the title Augustus, for it is derived from *augeo*, increase, and was felt to be related to *augurium*, augury. (He appears in the second half of *Julius Caesar* as a young man still known modestly under the name of Octavius.) The poetry, history, architecture and law of Rome, as they were practised under Augustus, became recognized as the very models of civilization itself. In our own day, to achieve status as a classic still implies permanent inalienable success. The images placed by advertisers in glossy magazines even in the late 1990s continue to incorporate pieces of classical sculpture. For an audience at the end of the twentieth century, which has unconsciously absorbed so much in the way of admiration for the products of Roman culture, it may be harder than it was for Shakespeare to bring scepticism to bear on the heritage of imperial Rome.

When people in Britain today speak the name of Julius Caesar, it is not always clear whether it's history or myth that they're talking about. This Roman soldier once landed his legions in Kent and forded the River Thames with his troops. It was with

Plate 2   Friends, Romans, Europeans: don't block your ears

On 29 March 1997 the *Economist* magazine ran this photograph of
European politicians, conferring at the foot of a statue from the Roman
past. Their caption uses an echo of Shakespeare's play to suggest that
listening to each other may not come easily to these men.

the arrival of Julius Caesar in these islands in 55 BCE, on a
mission of conquest that he recorded himself in his book *The
Gallic War*, that Britain entered the written record of Roman
history. It was a British scholar, interestingly enough, the Oxford
classicist Jasper Griffin, who described that book as 'the most
"masculine" work perhaps in all literature', a judgement that
openly invites readers to question their own notions of what it is
to be a man (HWC 15). Caesar's descriptions were drawn up
from the perspective of an invader: by the sixteenth century,
when Shakespeare was working in London, Caesar's practical
inventories were being used as a model by the conquistadores,
as they annexed South America for Spain.

It is unequivocally a matter of history that the life of Julius
Caesar came to an end in the city of Rome, when his friends fell
on him in broad daylight and stabbed him to death. That is the

story that we tell each other more often, the story that the British and other nations throughout Europe like to hear (see Plate 2). Perhaps we always hope that the next time we hear it we shall really understand. For the story of the decision to kill this one man, for the good of the people as his assassins argued, is the oldest and most respected tale of political life that is shared by the countries of Europe. It is as powerful as if it were not history but myth. In the modern imagination Caesar's death stands for the public and political order that we have inherited from Rome.

It might be time to remind ourselves that an earlier age could see things differently: writing on the cusp of the fourteenth century, the poet Dante set Brutus and Cassius to stand beside Judas Iscariot in the lowest circle of Hell. A new religion was being revealed, as his followers claimed, at the birth of Jesus, but it is a new political order that we trace back to the murder of Caesar, fifty years before. Maybe those events have more in common than first appears: for a start, they are not very far distant from each other in time. When the Roman empire collapsed five hundred years later, as historians tell us, it was Christianity that took over the administrative structures of government that Rome had left behind. I find myself asking today what Roman politics have meant for the values of modern Europe and I wonder whether a commentary on the beliefs and practices that make up the order of a Christian state at the end of the twentieth century can be found in Shakespeare's play of *Julius Caesar*. If we listen carefully to that story one more time, we might find a clue. Where did European civilization, the civilization that Europe still takes such pride in, start to go wrong?

2

Authority and Violence

'Hence! Home, you idle creatures, get you home!' (1.1.1). How angry and hectoring are the words which open the play. But Murellus and Flavius, the speakers, are tribunes of the people; that is, magistrates that the people have elected to protect their interests. As he takes the first step into the world which is moving towards the crisis of Caesar's death, Shakespeare chooses to invite us to make our own entrance, with him, at a point of collision. We are thrown immediately off-balance into confusion. Wanting to extricate ourselves from that, we might be tempted to suppress what as educated people we might be expected to know: that the tribunes are meant to be on the people's side. On the other hand these words might be a cue to us, as audience, to listen carefully, to be alert to the difference between what we see for ourselves and the official version of events. The magistrates are not protecting but attacking the commoners. It is sometimes argued that fear of the Elizabethan mob is what Shakespeare is dramatizing here in the clash between the tribunes and the common men who speak from the crowd. I suspect that to say this means that you have already aligned yourselves with the authorities and turned away from the common people in the scene. Let us try keeping a more open mind as we move forward into the world of the play.

What we are shown is a battle carried on in terms of language: the men of Rome are already fighting each other when the play begins. If it is a battle, since only one side is really on the attack. The tribunes are harrying the men that they have met with just for being out in the street. Who has a right to speak, what happens when people are silenced? These are questions that Shakespeare did not take from his source in Plutarch, just as he found no original there for his opening scene.' Cobblers, tapsters, or suchlike base mechanical people' (*JC* 164) was a phrase dismissively used by Cassius in Plutarch's *Life of Marcus Brutus*: on reading it perhaps Shakespeare balked. Out of that resistance, his refusal to recapitulate the casual disdain of that description, he may have forged his play.

The clash between tribunes and workmen is Shakespeare's invention: it is his decision also to make the quarrel one that takes place over language and what is sometimes known as signifying practice. 'Where is thy leather apron and thy rule?' (1.1.7). If they're out at all, the tribunes say, the workmen should be carrying the tools of their trade, as a sign of who they're supposed to be, or rather as a sign that simply identifies them with their work and with their inferior place as workers or plebeians in Rome. For Shakespeare's first audience this might have had a familiar ring, for their own government repeatedly passed laws that were intended to make their appearance reflect a particular social hierarchy. Sumptuary legislation under Elizabeth as it has been said 'dealt with every rung of the social ladder'.[1] It might be more accurate to say that sumptuary laws were an attempt to make English subjects believe in those rungs, those differences of status, and behave as if they were true. The story of Caesar tunes Shakespeare's imagination to the problems that hierarchy as a form of social organization entails. If by the same impulse he finds himself drawn to think about religious observance, this is not entirely a coincidence, for what else does the term hierarchy come from, according to the *Oxford English Dictionary*, but Greek words that mean the rule of priests?

It's as if the tribunes wanted to turn the workmen into images or signs without a voice. 'You blocks, you stones, you worse than senseless things!' Murellus scolds (1.1.34). He is comparing them to the statues in the great religious shrines, which had been a focus of devotional feeling until Henry VIII ordered that they should be destroyed after he took control of religion as head of the Church. Or rather, Shakespeare is striking a rhetorical note that his first audience would have recognized: he is echoing the regulatory voice of authority under its religious guise. The phrase 'blocks and stones', or more often 'stocks and stones', was used as the *OED* reminds us, in written texts to refer contemptuously to the old images of Mary and the saints. It is the ranting of religious authority, not its particular doctrines, that Shakespeare wants to reproduce here. This may seem to be Rome, he suggests, but you may find that it reminds you of what we have to put up with closer to home.

The tribune's voice, with its distinctive tone of authority, one that is at once insulting and intimate – notice how he uses the familiar form, calling the workmen 'thou' – is one that some of us may remember hearing from teachers at school. 'Don't you know that you're not allowed to do that?' they said. That may be where Shakespeare first heard it himself, at the grammar school in Stratford, where he learned his Latin. Shakespeare knew about the link between the Latin word *'magister'* meaning teacher and the English word 'magistrate'. It's an everyday kind of brainwashing that we observe, as Murellus, the magistrate who is supposed to support the commoners, humiliates them. It is done by rounding on their open, enthusiastic response and mocking it as irrational. The magistrates would like to put a stop to the life of impulse and replace self-respect in the commoners with a mechanical sense of themselves as inferior beings.

The tribunes don't seem to like spoken language or even to be competent in it themselves: the cobbler's quick replies baffle them 'What means't thou by that? Mend me, thou saucy fellow?' (1.1.18). You would almost think that in the presence of the play of language the tribunes feel afraid. They suspect that they can't quite follow what is going on. You do wonder yourself, when you hear the way that the tribunes use language when they want to persuade rather that to issue commands. It may be the day of Caesar's triumph, as the cobbler tells us, but we discover that the tribunes are hostile to Caesar as well as to the crowd. Does this suggest that it's the pleasure taken in Caesar that they want to destroy? The proper rules for a Roman triumph have not been observed they say. Perhaps the tribunes sense that a triumph mounted to celebrate the *defeat* of a Roman might put a spanner in the works, ruin the ideological effect, but this is not how they choose to frame their complaint. Instead they speak of the absence of foreign prisoners:

> Wherefore rejoice? What conquest brings he home?
> What tributaries follow him to Rome
> To grace in captive bonds his chariot wheels?

(1.1.31–3)

14

To grace in captive bonds his chariot wheels? Where do you begin arguing with a phrase like that? This is a speaker, or a member, as they say, of a speech community who seem to have decided to numb themselves. They do not feel the disjunction between the image of men in chains and the word 'grace', the language of religion or aesthetics. 'Grace' is not a term that most people would choose to apply to a man who is suffering. Most people find pain, whether in themselves or in others, hard to tolerate and neither holy nor beautiful; that is, unless they believe, like the Roman Catholic nuns who educated me, in meditating on the Passion of Christ. The artists of Christian Europe for centuries found inspiration in the suffering of Jesus, too. How many composers besides Handel wrote settings for *The Seven Last Words of Christ*? There may be more continuity and more sympathy between the order of Christianity and the order of ancient Rome than first appears.

In the lexicon of ancient Rome, as the tribunes are demonstrating, the dynamic that usually orders language does not apply. We sometimes speak of putting our feelings into words: in Rome, it seems, or in the official language of Rome, words are not found by paying attention to the way experience is registered within or to the resonances set up in the body by it. Shakespeare's habitual poetic unit, the iambic pentameter, has its source in the rhythms of the body: the time it takes to speak a pentameter is matched to the duration of a breath. But Murellus and Flavius don't use the sensitive pulse of their human response to pace their speech but a hammering mechanical beat that deadens the hearers as well. This makes it possible for Roman men to construct a new world, one that exists only in language and does not vibrate with reminders of the world of experience. With this denatured language it is easy to confuse and to lie and to construct a public world, a political world that is based in lies. Shakespeare opens his play by identifying the language of Roman officials as a problem and by offering that as the frame for the political crisis at hand. It might encourage us as his audience to wonder about patrician men and their refusal to connect the inner world with the outer one by means of language. What part will that refusal play in dividing Roman men against each other and against themselves?

Religion is supposed to hold a society together; the word

15

comes from Latin, either from *lego*, meaning gather, collect, or from *ligo*, meaning 'bind'. One way of doing this might be through weaving language into poems or histories or stories, either with the voice or in writing, making what we call a text. That word also comes from a Latin root, meaning 'tie'. But what the Romans bound together, famously, was a bundle of rods, in the symbol known as the fasces, that is the sign of the right to punish. Religion is already an issue as the play opens. It is in the name of religion that the workmen are told to get out of the public street:

> Run to your houses, fall upon your knees,
> Pray to the gods to intermit the plague
> That needs must light on this ingratitude.

> (1.1.52–4)

they are urged, in a speech that echoes the Act for the Uniformity of Common Prayer of 1559. Printed as the first item in the Prayer Book that members of Shakespeare's first audience used every week in church, this Act of Parliament spoke of 'evils and plagues wherewith Almighty God may justly punish his people' if they did not obey the queen's ordinance and present themselves every Sunday for worship.

The workmen are not to believe in themselves, as we have just learned; now we are told that they are to go in fear, a fear that the tribunes are also subject to, in their degree. The tribunes would like to remove all evidence of Caesar's popularity, and this would mean removing the offerings hung on his statues: 'Disrobe the images/If you do find them decked with ceremonies' (1.1.64), says Flavius. It makes Murellus hesitate, for there are laws about what you do with statues, it seems. Plutarch had said that diadems, broad metal bands worn by kings, had been hung on Caesar's statues but Shakespeare refuses that cue. Hanging the statues at shrines with votive gifts had been an important part of English religious practice: as Shakespeare's audience would have known, those old statues would have been hung with wax crutches, or other symbols of the healing that the sick came to find there; that audience might have picked up too a familiar word in the phrase 'decked with ceremonies'.[2] If we find the phrase awkward as modern readers and notice as we go on that the word 'ceremonies' is made prominent twice more in the play

16

– Caesar has come to rely on 'ceremonies' (2.1.197), Calpurnia 'never stood on ceremonies' (2.2.13) – it could be that we are picking up a trail that has been deliberately laid.

Arguments about religion in England in the sixteenth century centre on what are acceptable 'ceremonies' as much as they do on matters of doctrine: Elizabeth's Prayer Book was prefaced by a note 'Of ceremonies, why some be abolished and some retained'. It was with threats of punishment, of plague sent by God or fines from the crown that Elizabeth used that Prayer Book to impose herself as ruler, to control and standardize her subjects' experience. Behind the figure of the magistrate/teacher, that we have already identified in the tribunes, does there lurk a priest? With its spies and its censorship Elizabeth's England was close to being a police state: historians agree that independence of thought was extremely dangerous. Shakespeare had need to be cautious, for there were heavy penalties for any criticism of the Prayer Book or of its provisions, whether made in 'any interludes, plays, songs rhymes or by other open words'.[3] Shakespeare is writing about a world of fear but he knows enough to keep himself out of danger: without ever putting a Roman priest, much less a cleric of the Church of England, on the stage, he prepares to encourage his audience to share his scepticism about the state and about the religion that it sponsors.

There is something furtive about the tribunes, something that we might almost call conspiratorial, as they plan to sabotage the celebration of Caesar's triumph. Their language has shifted out of the official register of 1.1.30–59, with its remorseless pounding, into something more fluid, more like the way the workmen spoke. But what has made these officers so afraid that they turn to each other in private to share their fear, to plot and even to reach for a language that will give the fear a name? Shakespeare creates a form of speech for Flavius as a Roman that he will return to again in this play, the voice of a man speaking in private who is able to indicate his desire, in this case the will to make Caesar appear less exceptional, without naming it directly or being able to resist justifying his wish.

> These growing feathers plucked from Caesar's wing
> Will make him fly an ordinary pitch,
> Who else would soar above the view of men
> And keep us all in servile fearfulness.

> (1.1.71–5)

he argues. Paradoxically, it seems to be envy that has made these Roman magistrates sound more human. It makes Flavius feel as humiliated as one of the workmen to be so outclassed. No wonder audiences find *Julius Caesar* a puzzling play if they come expecting to admire Roman heroes.

When modern scholars write about the man who was Julius Caesar, they may situate him with other able young aristocrats in Rome, like Sulla and Catiline, who had the intelligence to observe those weaknesses in the political system which offered them the opportunity of gaining power for themselves (*HWC*). But even those who are consciously avoiding adulation acknowledge that Caesar's clear vision, his energy and his decisiveness really were quite out of the ordinary. By the time of his death, though, Caesar had aggregated power to himself in defiance of the Roman constitution: in the words of Jasper Griffin, 'accepting unheard of titles, unconstitutional magistracies, the right to wear extraordinary dress, the right to nominate the consuls, statues everywhere, an ivory image to be paraded with those of the gods...' (HWC 18). The Greeks had a word for it, as we say; they would have condemned this as *hubris*, the desire to see oneself as more than human, not governed by the limitations shared by other human beings. That desire doesn't seem to have been conceptualized as a risky one in Rome. The tension between these public assertions of greatness and the frailty of Caesar as merely human will be put by Shakespeare under deliberate strain in his play. There is a madness, a nonsense at the centre of the public stage in Rome, which other leading men cannot help but perceive, though they may lack the words to name what is disturbing them. In their confusion, where will they resort but to violence?

Julius Caesar himself does not appear on the stage until the play has already signalled the death of language and the demand for obedience in Rome. When he does make his entrance, at the head of a train, it is clear that his is the voice of supreme authority. The first word that Caesar utters on this very public occasion is the name of his wife, Calpurnia. Caesar has instructions to give Calpurnia, or is it an order? She answers to her name like a schoolchild at roll-call: 'Here, my lord' (1.2.2).

> Stand you directly in Antonio's way
> When he doth run his course. Antonio.

> (1.2.3–4)

18

Caesar doesn't even devote a complete breath to his wife but passes on to his friend before the line finishes. When Lear wanted to make public proof of his daughters' obedience he was lucky enough to find one who would offer him resistance, but Lear was not living in a Roman world; there is no such bracing opposition for Caesar, 'When Caesar says "Do this", it is performed' (1.2.10), Antony emphasizes flatteringly. Or should we in the audience be taking Shakespeare's cue and calling him 'Antonio', thinking of him as a seventeenth-century Roman, not an ancient one? As spectators we may already be wondering about Shakespeare's choice. Why present Caesar exercising authority over his wife while showing him at the same time in interaction with his friend?

It is difficult to say whether it is Caesar's weakness or his power that is more emphasized by Shakespeare in this scene. There is more than a suggestion of personal vulnerability in the way that he is presented. Casca has to call for silence when he speaks, which implies to us that Caesar's own voice is not strong. Nobody calls for silence so that Lear can be heard. And Caesar's own hearing is poor, he doesn't catch the voice of the Soothsayer at first. 'Ha? Who calls?' (1.2.13) he asks and Casca is obliged to ask for silence a second time. It was Plutarch, following the historical record, who reported that Caesar was deaf but it was Shakespeare the playwright who chose to make a prominent feature of this disability. When the actor says 'Speak, Caesar is turned to hear' (1.2.17), he is obliged to mime with his whole body, in turning towards the source of sound, the action of a man whose sight and hearing are weak, the action of a man who has trouble, perhaps, in following what is going on.

'Beware', is the message of the Soothsayer: in Rome it is proper to be afraid. For Caesar too? Even for Caesar himself? But Caesar is blank at the suggestion that there might be a place for fear. 'He is a dreamer' (1.2.24), he dismisses the Soothsayer and sweeps on. It would be easy to label this moment as 'dramatic irony' and by doing so to risk blurring its specific effect. Let's not make that move: instead, let us register that virtually every time this scene is played the entire audience knows that the Soothsayer is correct, that his warning is exact and timely. This also means that each audience observes that Caesar turns his back on clarity and exposes himself to danger. Haven't we met other senior Romans

19

in this play who have trouble picking up what's said to them? The tribunes are one with Caesar in this respect. Some people might think that Caesar's rebuff to the Soothsayer means that he is brave in a special dignified Roman way, but Shakespeare's play does not support such a simple endorsement. By making Caesar deaf, both literally and figuratively to the voice of warning, Shakespeare's dramatic framing suggests that there is danger, danger and foolhardiness in the ways of Rome.

Nothing is more open to question than the way her husband treated Calpurnia at the start of the scene. Though as we shall see later, in Act 3, Caesar is not a specially unkind or distant husband in private, when it comes to his public relations with Calpurnia he assumes indifference to her feelings, as if they did not exist. Many readers have followed the play using the same model. Such readers will ignore Calpurnia's feelings too. They will explain that Shakespeare intended to indicate by this scene in Act 1 that Caesar wanted a son in order to establish a dynasty; they will say that the playwright was offering evidence that Caesar wanted to be king. The temptation to 'prove' that Caesar deserved to die, to join the party of the conspirators, as it were, is one to resist in my view.

It seems more responsive to what Shakespeare actually chooses to show us, to note that in this scene Calpurnia is isolated and subjected to public disgrace, when her infertility is paraded in the street, a disgrace that is presented as routine and associated with a religious ceremony. Shakespeare places this scene right up front at the start of the action, where it cannot be missed. Does he want us to start thinking about marriage and the way that Roman men, or even contemporary ones, treat their wives? *Julius Caesar* does not end with the assassination of a single hero; that takes place only halfway through. The action of this play makes a connection between that one carefully justified killing and the confused violence of warfare in which the men who argued for Caesar's death are swept away. Though *Julius Caesar* apparently concerns itself so little with women – it's such a male play, as is often said – from the moment that Caesar is actually on stage our attention as audience is directed to the figure of a woman, standing silent at the hub of Rome. None of us, least of all her husband, knows what she is thinking. What would happen if she brought her voice into the conspiracies of Rome?

20

3

Women – or Statues?

Julius Caesar may end in war, but it opens in celebrations. As an artist, Shakespeare chooses to run the military occasion of the triumph and the religious one together on the stage, making an overt connection for his audience between the two. When Caesar enters, accompanied by friends and followed by a crowd, his movements are accompanied by sennets or fanfares. There may be no lights or statues, the usual features of church processions in the Rome of our own day, but there is no doubt that in the public spaces of ancient Rome a religious ritual is being observed. We have already been told by the tribunes that this day of festival is called Lupercal. Is that a day for worshipping Caesar, one might ask, in some sense that is not quite obvious at first? Instead of effigies or statues there are living bodies, specially selected ones, that are marked out to be the focus of ritual and of our attention as audience. These bodies seem almost to emerge from that dream of Julius Caesar which we found interfused in *Hamlet*. One of them is a silent woman, fully clothed; the other, a male one, is nearly naked: the directions say that Antony is stripped 'for the course': he's going running.

This tableau offers a powerful juxtaposition, a stage image that might prompt us as readers and critics to pause. We might decide to ask ourselves about the work that it is doing in the play. First the tribunes wanted to reduce the workmen to silence, to make them into signs or ciphers of the labour they performed, now we find Caesar ordering his wife to stand like a statue and wait. Was there a resonance that Shakespeare picked up, something he recognized in Plutarch's description of the Lupercalia, that chimed with the notes that he had already begun to strike himself in this play? Or to put it another way, was there a critique of Rome already implicit in Plutarch's

21

language that Shakespeare was only taking up and giving amplification? Editors have often stressed how faithfully he can follow Plutarch. Let's reread for ourselves what North's version of Plutarch told him.

> At that time the feast Lupercalia was celebrated, the which in old time men say was the feast of shepherds or herdmen and is much like unto the feast of the Lycians in Arcadia. But, howsoever it is, that day there are divers noblemen's sons, young men – and some of them magistrates themselves that govern then – which run naked through the city, striking in sport them they meet in their way with leather thongs, hair and all on, to make them give place. And many noblewomen and gentlewomen also go of purpose to stand in their way, and do put forth their hands to be stricken, as scholars hold them out to their schoolmaster to be stricken with the ferula; persuading themselves that, being with child, they shall have good delivery, and also, being barren, that it will make them to conceive with child. Caesar sat to behold that sport upon the pulpit for orations, in a chair of gold, apparelled in triumphing manner. (*JC* 156)

Plutarch is writing about a public occasion, something like a pageant, in which history is replayed and at the same time the structures of both religious and civil authority are acted out. When they want to reassert the values that Britain stands for, a modern government prescribes that schoolchildren shall study the story of Julius Caesar, perhaps even see that story performed on stage, but in Rome they looked back to the story of Romulus and Remus. They professed to believe that the origins of the Lupercalia lay beyond the reach of memory or history – could it have started somewhere among the shepherds of Greece? – but the story that the ceremony pointed to was based closer to home.

Some of the men who run in the Lupercalia, as Plutarch reports, are magistrates, so what they do is associated with the force of law. But this law is one that goes otherwise unwritten. It concerns relations between women and men of the governing class. In the Lupercalia the sons of the ruling classes are called on to discipline and subordinate women of their own rank. Was it in Plutarch's image of the schoolmaster that Shakespeare recognized the exercise of power, or was it in his description of Caesar as half conqueror and half priest? In the play of *Julius Caesar*, Shakespeare had begun by asking about authority and Roman men; the ritual of the Lupercalia offered him an image of the place given to women in Rome.

Taking part in rituals is sometimes known as observing them: the performance of the Lupercalia was meant to tell on spectators as well as on those who were educated by taking part. In his book *How Societies Remember*, Paul Connerton argues that spectacles of this sort, staged displays in the public spaces of the city, are the way that human societies make sure that what is important is remembered.[1] Knowledge of this kind, he maintains, is directly conveyed by such means into the body, without the medium of language. For us though, contemplating the Lupercalia as it is put into drama for us by Shakespeare, the wordless spectacle of the two bodies is framed by language. We are invited to think for ourselves about what is going on, to join him in wondering what is at stake when Roman men set up women as passive and silent, mere voiceless images, to invite aggression in the streets of Rome.

Modern reference books, issued by the university presses, that we turn to as scholars for guidance can tell us even more about the Lupercalia, though they may not approach it with the scepticism of Shakespeare's play. That dissenting note will have to be struck by ourselves. From the *Oxford Companion to Classical Literature* we learn that the Lupercalia, the holy race that Antony is about to take part in was 'a very ancient festival at Rome, held on 15 February' every year.[2] The Lupercalia seemed designed to remind Romans of the terms on which their city was founded and perhaps also of what it meant to be a Roman man. Young men, selected from 'particular families', set out from a cave in which according to legend Romulus and Remus, the founders of the city, were suckled by a she-wolf (*OCCL*). In the cave before the race began two goats and one dog were killed. Anthropologists encourage us to take such rituals seriously, to read them as evidence of the way that societies structure their beliefs and their lives. It was in Britain just prior to the First World War that Jane Ellen Harrison, the classical scholar, pioneered the interpretation of the material culture of ancient Greece. If we ask today about the ritual of the Lupercalia, what shall we find? Could it be a renewed attempt, annually performed in ritual, to emphasize the difference between male and female, to break the connection between the maternal body and the male children that it had fed? From its very beginnings Rome had disclaimed that connection by asserting that its founders were men who had been nursed by a mother that was not human.

The runners chosen to commemorate that story and to represent those founding fathers ran a course that took them out of the cave and round the Palatine Hill, the site of the original settlement of Rome. They were smeared with blood from the sacrificed animals and ran dressed in the skins of the goats, with strips of goats' hide, which were known as *februa* or 'means of purification', in their hands. 'Women placed themselves on their course to receive blows from these thongs', as the reference books tell us, but it might be more realistic to say that Roman women complied with the instruction to stand there inviting a blow (*OCCL*). It is claimed that this was done 'to procure fertility'. To a sceptical reader at the end of the twentieth century, as it did to Plutarch earlier, with his talk of school-masters, it sounds rather as if the women were being symbolically punished. Or were they even being threatened with violence? The young men were, after all, streaked with fresh blood.

At the Lupercalia, as I would argue, a lesson was being repeated in the exchange between women and men of the governing class, the patrician order in Rome. A warning, perhaps, about the closeness between them that sexual intimacy might entail. The only women who would have put themselves forward in the course of this ritual, let us be clear, would have been those who were married. The purification administered by those strips of goathide called *februa* was designed to undo a pollution: perhaps the emotional and physical intimacy of marriage was the danger here. Or was the Lupercalia performed for the benefit of Roman men, as a reminder that their only human likeness was to be found in the bodies of other men, that as men they were something quite different from the women who had borne them and from those who shared their lives? First drawing and then maintaining a distinction between women and men, the creation of gender difference as we have learned to call it, is a fundamental principle in organising human society and not only in the west. The month in which the Lupercalia took place was named *februarius*, after the februa, the strips of goathide used in the ceremony; there was no uncertainty about the importance of 'purification', of keeping the sexes distinct and apart from each other in ancient Rome.

Shakespeare's England had its ceremonies of purification too. The new Prayer Book issued under Elizabeth included a ceremony known as churching to mark the reappearance of women after they had given birth. Purity is a word that Christian rhetoric has set great store by, also making a connection between purity and keeping the sexes apart. The unexpected consistency between ancient practices and modern ones might lead us to think again about the Christian virtue of purity and the purposes it has served. Are they really so different from the pagan ones from antiquity, we might ask? It's a serious question: through the form of his drama Shakespeare has urged us to accept that its action, one of escalating politically motivated violence between men, is rooted in the moment of the Lupercalia in Rome, if not generated by that ceremony.

'The feast of Lupercal' as it is described in the play is a phrase that sounds as Christian as it does Roman; the feast of Stephen, in the words of the Christmas carol means the day that St Stephen is honoured. If we can't find the day that the Lupercalia is honoured in the Christian calendar, maybe we should try substituting for it a feast that Shakespeare himself knew well, the feast of Candlemas. Though it is not so universally observed in Britain as it once was, Candlemas was one of the most important festivals of the year, bound up, as the OED tells us, with the offices of education, the state and public life. 'It had been time out of mind celebrated at court with more than ordinary solemnity', as l'Estrange the diarist was noting in 1655. In 1857 Candlemas was still a holiday in the public offices, while in Scotland it used to mark the quarter day and was one of the dates for paying school fees.

Candlemas and Lupercal have more in common than one might have thought. They exhibit an impressive continuity. Both were performed in the same month, for Candlemas fell on the second day of February, the month that still bore the name of the *februa*. Like the pagan festival of the Lupercalia, the Christian festival was one of purification, the purification of the Virgin Mary. In fact, the two festivals were linked historically, for the Lupercalia had kept on being performed right into Christian times. It was 494 CE when the Bishop of Rome ordained that the celebration of the Lupercalia should be assimilated to the

Christian festival of the Purification of the Virgin Mary after the birth of Christ. What did the Virgin need to be purified from, anyone might be forgiven for asking? When I was a girl in school I was taught that in going through the purification ceremony Mary, who was a Jewish woman, was demonstrating her submission to her own religion and its law, but now that I have lived for fifty years in the world as a woman myself I suspect that, for Christians, celebrating Mary's purification had another meaning, one that was unacknowledged and unvoiced. It kept alive the distinction between the mother's body and the body of the son that was marked in pagan Rome by the feast of Lupercal. For Mary, like the she-wolf, had got too close for comfort to the sacred male figure.

That bold invention at the start of 1.2, where the ageing Caesar stands by the naked figure of Antony the young man and authorizes him to lift his hand against Caesar's own wife, offers us a highly condensed image, like a dream. Or should we name this dream as a nightmare instead? A nightmare that tells us of collusion between older men and younger ones entered into against women, a familiar nightmare that we have domesticated under the name of patriarchy. The Lupercalia teaches women to accept humiliation in public. Shakespeare's drama asks us as his audience to pause and to recognize that ceremony as one that has an affinity with marriage, the Christian marriage that was enforced in the England of his own experlence.

Portia enters the stage at the same time as does Calpurnia, following Caesar, but they do not speak to each other at 1.2. If directors make them gossip together in dumb show they may be missing the point or rather failing to mark the silence between women that is suggested in this play. Shakespeare stages no occasion where women talk with each other in the city of Rome. The symbolic isolation imposed on Calpurnia as exemplary wife in the Lupercalia is carried seamlessly into practice for all women, as we realize when at last we are called on to share the experience of a woman, when we meet Portia, the wife of Brutus. Not until the second act do we hear a woman's voice utter anything but a pledge of obedience. In public Calpurnia answered to her husband with the docility of a child but when we encounter Portia at 2.1.233, she is on home territory and she does not wait to be called. We could choose to spend time in discussing the differences between the women in this play, in drawing distinctions between them. I don't think that that's a helpful thing to do, it's too close to the Roman injunction to keep women apart from each other for my taste. Why join in the work of Roman authority, so concerned as it is with marking distinctions? That plays down or in the end even breaks the connections between people, obscuring all that they hold in common. Instead, let us concentrate on the situation that these two women share, their situation, first as women, then as the wives of Roman men.

A French anthropologist, Claude Lévi-Strauss, once defined women as objects of exchange between men; it was a French woman, the philosopher Luce Irigaray, who retorted that such a view of women could only survive as long as women did not speak to each other. Portia and Calpurnia share their predicament as women who speak but cannot be heard, because there is no other woman present to hear and to support what they say. This can make them both sound crazy, to an audience and to themselves. It is up to us, though, as hearers primed by Shakespeare's scrupulous scene-setting, to listen for the effects of that isolation and humiliation of wives we have seen institutionalized in the name of religion in Rome. Lest you should misunderstand me, it is the state as the play argues, not individual men that underwrites this work of discipline, as I repeat. What can we hear of that experience in their voices, when Calpurnia and Portia attempt to speak and address their husbands?

Let us take our time in considering what Shakespeare chooses to show about husbands and wives in *Julius Caesar*, reading through all the scenes where Roman marriage is staged. We are after all being invited to understand how the most intimate relationship between women and men plays into the civil violence towards which the action is moving. Or, to put it another way, Shakespeare is suggesting that we should situate the killing of Caesar, a husband, in relation to the suicide of Portia, a wife who dies near the close of the play. By the institution of marriage, so the play suggests, women are disciplined and schooled to behave as if they're different from men, even if they can't always bring themselves quite to accept what they've been taught. 'Nor for yours neither', says Portia, coming on the scene to challenge Brutus (2.1.237). Nothing can quite flatten out the shock, the near-impertinence of her quick rejoinder to his kindly reproof: 'It is not for your health thus to commit/Your weak condition to the raw cold morning' (2.1.235–6): do we hear the faintest echo of the public threat against women confusingly transmuted into husbandly concern here? Portia certainly seems to reply as though she were stung. Can a wife be impertinent to a husband? Aren't they equals, isn't that what we like to think? But a tiny insistent echo of hierarchy resisted, disrupted, lingers, however many times we repeat the retort to ourselves. No matter how tenderly the actress may choose to speak the words, Portia is reminding Brutus not to imagine that he is any different from her. Critics who would like to see in this marriage an ideal that Shakespeare is holding up for our admiration can only do so by not paying attention to what passes between husband and wife here. In the scene between Portia and Brutus it is the deformations imposed by Roman marriage that are being staged.

The matter was never one of merely antiquarian interest. The structure of marriage, or rather the structure of authority within marriage was not very different in Shakespeare's England from what it was in Caesar's Rome, in fact it might just as well have the title of Roman marriage, since the institution had been set up by the Roman church and set up rather late in the day, as you might say. Not until the thirteenth century did the church begin to insist that heterosexual coupling should be brought under ecclesiastical authority and to claim it as a sacrament, that is as an 'outward sign of inward spiritual grace', a kind of language that might remind us of the invocation of the Great Chain of Being. Before that time couples were free to ask a blessing on their union or not as they felt inclined. The invention of 'the sacrament of marriage' allowed the authority of the church to be extended more minutely into women's lives. By means of their most intimate desires, women were grappled more firmly into a structure of authority ruled by men. This became much clearer after the Reformation, when the monasteries were closed down and the single life for both women and men was discredited (see plate 3). From then on marriage was imposed as a new uniformity; 'compulsory heterosexuality', as Adrienne Rich has

Plate 3   Pope Julius II as Caesar

This image, created in Augsburg in 1521, is a visual pun; it was offered
in illustration of an account of Julius Caesar's love for Cleopatra, but it
also makes reference to issues that were contemporary for the artist.
Caesar is wearing the papal tiara and carrying the keys of St Peter, in a
reminder of Pope Julius II (d. 1513) who liked to be thought of as a
second Caesar. The image as a whole addresses the new enforcement of
marriage that was already taking place in the city.
See *Signs of Cleopatra*, ch. 2.

named it, was still something of a novelty when Shakespeare
wrote. The superiority of the husband was self-evident, to most
contemporary theory at least, which is hardly surprising since an
important effect of readopting the classical tradition was to
strengthen all forms of authority, as historians agree. During the
sixteenth century, ninety per cent of the population in England
was married, so it has been claimed, so ninety per cent of women
were formally subordinated to a man. For Shakespeare, to
investigate the order of marriage was a logical extension of his
enquiry into the political organization of the state.

4

Portia and Calpurnia

When Portia enters and starts to speak, it is the first time, as we realize, that the voice of a woman has been heard. In public Calpurnia expressed only acquiescence and stood silent. Or perhaps we haven't even thought that was odd, for to some people the life we are shown in Shakespeare's Rome is perfectly natural and of interest only because it is such a good imitation of normal behaviour as we meet it in real life, rather than Shakespeare's play being a way of confronting us with questions about what we now think is normal and about what we take for granted.

To a woman's ear, the ear of a woman who has been married more than once, as I have, and as indeed the historical Portia herself had been, the words of Brutus strike a familiar note. The wife takes her husband by surprise; 'What are you doing here?' he asks, rather put out as the broken movement of his first line shows: 'Portia! What mean you? Wherefore rise you now?' (2.1.233). As a form of greeting this leaves something to be desired, the more so perhaps if we hear in it a muted and domestic echo of the tribunes' cry that opened the play: 'Hence! home, you idle creatures, get you home!' (1.1.1.). Even at home there is a Roman official alert to maintain control of the space. Though Brutus goes on more smoothly, a wife might well hear reproof in his voice, under the even movement of the iambics, a reproof offered under the guise of telling Portia what is good for her. 'It is not for your health thus to commit/Your weak condition to the raw cold morning.' (2.1.235–6), warns Brutus, reminding his· wife to think of herself as weak. If instructing Portia offers a way for Brutus to stabilize himself, after the interview with the conspirators who have only just left the stage, for Portia to answer him with 'Nor for yours neither' breaks through that temporary calm. 'Nor for yours neither', she tells him, reminding him that what is bad for her is also bad for him, that she is not the only one who might fall sick. That a man's body is not that different from a woman's, after all. If nearly everyone in this play is sick in some way as Wilson Knight suggested – Caesar suffers from epilepsy and deafness, Brutus claims to be out of sorts, Ligarius is too ill to attend the conspirators' meeting, while Calpurnia has not been able to conceive and Portia mutilates herself – perhaps we are now being shown the common source of the diseases of *Julius Caesar*, a source that is found in the relations between women and men.[1]

The conspirators wanted Brutus to act but Portia, his wife, wants him to speak to her. 'Speak to me speak, why do you never speak', begs the woman in T. S. Eliot's poem *The Waste Land*. Does Portia sound like that in the ears of Brutus? But such terms as neurasthenic or neurotic, which are often applied to the anxious women in Eliot, don't seem to fit the behaviour of Portia here. As she speaks, she reveals herself, in Carol Gilligan's phrase as 'a naturalist of the human world' in her close observation of her husband. Maybe this is not what a Roman wife was supposed to do. It was Virginia Woolf, wasn't it, who suggested that for hundreds of years women had had the magic power of reflecting men at twice their natural size?[2] When Portia mirrors Brutus in this play, she does not show him what he wants to see about himself or reach for the language of admiration used to him by other men.

> yesternight at supper
> You suddenly arose and walked about,
> Musing and sighing, with your arms across,
> And when I asked you what the matter was,
> You stared upon me with ungentle looks.
> I urged you further, then you scratched your head
> And too impatiently stamped with your foot.
> Yet I insisted, yet you answered not,
> But with an angry wafture of your hand
> Gave sign for me to leave you.

(2.1.238–47)

It does not please Brutus to be observed in this state, reduced to silence, a silence that makes him strangely akin to the speechless bodies that Rome would like to make of the workmen and of the women, capable only of making a wordless gesture, a sign. For all her training as a Roman wife, Portia cannot avoid registering his behaviour in fine detail and noting it as strange. Case notes are what Portia offers, a scrupulous record of the recent interaction between them, which has convinced her that he is in distress.

When the resemblance was noted between the symptoms of shell-shock in army officers during the First World War and the hysteria that Freud had studied in intelligent highly educated women, W. H. R. Rivers offered an explanation.[3] Rivers suggested that when the officers found themselves trapped and made helpless by the conditions of trench warfare, that put them into a position more often occupied by women, who in everyday life found themselves the targets of external attacks against which they had no defence. Men of other ranks manifested the same symptoms too. What if the problem for Brutus was his position as a man, a man confined by the language that Rome with its particular values and traditions made available to him? There might be more to men and to women too than their culture chose to recognize. Portia's description of the gesticulating, frowning body of her husband might well put us in mind today of the distorted postures adopted by hysterics that were recorded in the photographs of Charcot (*FM* 149–54). Aphasia is the term used for the loss of speech but it sounds very clinical. Showing Brutus utterly speechless might have suggested that, like Ophelia in *Hamlet*, he was abnormally disturbed. But that is not at all Shakespeare's point here. Brutus is nothing if not a normal and decent man. Instead Shakespeare chooses to ask us as audience to believe the words of Portia, when she tells us that Brutus is moved by feelings that he cannot put into speech.

We are to believe Portia, though we may come to be troubled by the excess of her own emotion as the scene proceeds, an excess that produces not speechlessness but a flood of language, too many words. 'I am not well in health, and that is all.' (2.1.257), mutters Brutus, almost sulkily. Isn't physical illness what hysterics turn to when they cannot reach language? Brutus might sound composed, to some ears, when he claims that he is simply not well but the audience knows for itself and Shakespeare is exploiting this, to drive a wedge between Brutus and ourselves, that this composure is a false front, a mask.

Strange that some of us should feel as audience that there is something dignified about his lie; we may be closer to ancient Rome still than we think – or than Shakespeare was. The masks of ancestors were kept in the homes of certain Roman aristocrats and worn on the streets on special days: is it part of the duty of a Roman, even of a modern one, to keep the truth about himself from his wife? If Portia begins to sound insistent and even hysterical herself as she tries to make sense of him, if she kneels and starts to beg to be allowed to know what is happening in her own house, can we listening to her put a name to her desperation?

Deprivation or denial of sensory input can drive people mad. If hysteria develops when women or men are under threat and unable to defend themselves, there might be a threat to Portia that we need to recognize. It might lie in her husband, Brutus, in his refusal to acknowledge his own disturbance, a fact that she cannot avoid knowing because she's so close to him.

> You have some sick offence within your mind,
> Which by the right and virtue of my place
> I ought to know of.

> (2.1.268–70)

Portia begs. That right and virtuous place, Roman marriage, whose rules both Brutus and Portia are earnestly trying to observe, seems to be almost a form of torture for both women and men and to come between them at every turn. Portia has begun to frame questions about marriage for herself; is it because she is a wife that her husband must keep himself secret from her, she wonders?

> Within the bond of marriage, tell me, Brutus,
> Is it excepted I should know no secrets
> That appertain to you?

> (2.1.280–82)

Her husband never has to address this question, because it is immediately translated or transposed by Portia, who is a good daughter of Rome, into a complaint.

Like Freud's patients, and like the women Virginia Woolf wrote of, Portia was one of the daughters of educated men, 'excellently well seen in philosophy' as Plutarch writes, but this may not have been much help to her (*JC* 166). Her own father, Cato, who is said to have spent the last night before he killed himself reading Plato, is also described in the same entry as being impervious to reason (*OCCL*). Portia too is trapped within the structures of Roman thought. A good woman, as Portia has been told, is a wife: a bad one a harlot. Stop treating me like a bad woman, she says, instead of staying with the all-important question: can it really be true that good women are meant to be punished by being kept at a distance by their husbands?

Though Portia can move Brutus to feeling – usually by physical gestures like kneeling rather than by words – she cannot move him to a language that escapes from the shackles of Rome. He can only repeat that she is true and honourable, a Roman wife and not a Roman harlot. The division between good women and bad ones seems the only way of thinking about women that is of interest in Rome. If Brutus tells Portia that she is dear to him, as he does, he phrases it in terms of comparing her to his blood. Perhaps Portia also thinks that only deep in the body, where the response to experience and to the outside world can remain locked and unspoken within living tissue, can what is true and what is valuable be found. Portia cut into her own body – 'Giving myself a voluntary wound/Here, in the thigh.' (2.1.300–301) – in order to convince Brutus of her own worth, a worth that would be identical with silence, with keeping silent about her husband. A Roman wife must keep quiet about what she knows.

Portia cuts herself: when women do that today it is taken as a sign that they are gravely at risk, as the work of psychiatrist Estela Welldon has shown.[4] You would not think any husband or lover could bear to see his wife's body mutilated in this way. But Brutus exclaims in admiration at the wound: 'O ye gods,/Render me worthy of this noble wife!' (2.1.302–3). What gods would prompt a man to admire a wounded body? It is earthly powers that profit from the battles where wounds are received. But in a military culture like Rome's, that is one that makes waging war the principle by which it grows, the human instinct to recoil from injury has to be managed and transformed. In the course of her good Roman education, Portia has learned the same lessons that are designed to form Roman men. When it comes to bodies, there has been an attempt to educate both Brutus and Portia out of tenderness and respect. But perhaps in a Roman marriage, as in a

34

Roman Catholic one today, where control of fertility is officially forbidden, husband and wife are not intended to be lovers. There is sadness in those words that Portia utters soon after she begins to address her husband; 'Y'have ungently, Brutus,/Stole from my bed' (2.1.237–8), she complains. Is it tenderness and sexual pleasure that Portia is missing?

There was a market for images of Portia making demonstration of the wound in her thigh, in Christian Europe after the Renaissance (see plate 4). They seem to have been intended to titillate, as the image of a sexualized wound. Maybe this image of Portia offers a surrogate, suggesting that the vagina is a wound, one that might be made or probed by a blade. Bodies are so exciting to each other: it seems that pleasure in active cruelty must develop once tenderness for the body has been discredited and disallowed. Freud argued that men could not bear to look directly at representations of the female genital because it reminded them that their own member could be cut off, but the image of Portia and the example of Freud himself might seem to expand that theory.[5] What if the imaginary, the unconscious of Christian Europe, were haunted by the image of the vagina as a wound, a wound that might have given pleasure to someone in making it?

Portia is at risk both physically and psychologically: we are left in no doubt of this by the demonstration of her anxiety at 2.4 when she is waiting to discover whether the attack on Caesar has been carried out. Her breathing, the process by which she maintains the exchange of oxygen in her body, has become uneven as the jerky line-movement reveals:

> I prithee, boy, run to the Senate House.
> Stay not to answer me but get thee gone.
> Why dost thou stay?

> (2.4.1–3)

Of course the scene in one sense is playing with the audience, who are being teased and made to wait for the climactic moment of the murder. The appetite in us for violence is being worked up. But there is something for us to learn about Portia, something we need to understand. We might be tempted to compare her with Lady Macbeth, another wife in a warrior culture who decides that she must stop being a woman. Lady

Plate 4 *Portia Wounding her Thigh*, 1664 by Elisabetta Sirani 1638–65.

Plutarch's text specifies a wound in the thigh but artists rarely ventured to show one made any higher than the knee – compare frontispiece – as if Plutarch's image, once given visual form, would be too graphic a reminder of the vagina.

Macbeth, who tells us that she has borne children, wants to suppress her milk, to undo what is maternal in her response and in her body. It is a move, as we know, that would be appreciated in Rome. But Portia, the educated woman, the woman who has had the intellectual training of a Roman man, is required to suppress her own voice.

> O constancy, be strong upon my side,
> Set a huge mountain 'tween my heart and tongue!
> I have a man's mind, but a woman's might.
> How hard it is for women to keep counsel!–

> (2.4.6–9)

Portia finds herself put under unexpected pressure once she is more closely involved in public affairs: her anxiety must be kept secret. Being true to Brutus and true to her education for Portia means learning to block her own response and to silence herself. Intuitively though, she knows the enormity of what she has undertaken and names it in the imagery of her speech. Agreeing to suppress her own voice means introducing a stony mass into the living organism of her body, a mass that will crush out her life. We have seen her put up one fight against the demand to suppress her own perceptions and her fears, when she succeeded in persuading Brutus to confide in her. Portia wanted only to share more closely in her husband's life. Now we realize that the demand for self-censorship in women was one that Portia has absorbed into her own being. Portia's training in dissociation began when her education divided her from herself, teaching her to believe that she had 'a man's mind but a woman's might'. She is proud of being able to think like a Roman man, and even to speak as if she were one, against her own sex: 'How hard it is for women to keep counsel' she moralizes. This means that when actively suppressing her voice makes her feel ill – 'I must go in.' (2.4.39), 'O, I grow faint–.' (2.4.43) – instead of pausing to question what she is doing to herself as a woman, Portia falls back on the adages she has been taught. She has only just admitted that it will take the weight of a 'huge mountain' to prevent the impulses of her heart from issuing in speech when Portia laments 'Ay me, how weak a thing/The heart of woman is!' (2.4.39–40). As Shakespeare's audience, we can hear Portia contradict herself and enter into

37

confusion: to us Portia's problem appears to be that her impulses, her feelings of anxiety on behalf of her husband at this critical moment are so strong. Portia may think of herself as failing but we who observe her recognize a triumph, the triumph of her Roman education in Portia. This education has taught her to despise what she feels as a woman and has cut her off from the promptings of her own voice. Nothing in that education prepared her to recognize when she was putting herself in danger.

Two acts later at 4.3 Shakespeare shows us what is the outcome when a woman educated in Rome is put under the double stress of sharing the tensions of her husband's life. The news of Portia's suicide comes to us at the close of a quarrel between her husband and his friend and on the eve of the battle between men that will take up the whole last act of the play. Portia's death cannot be separated from the struggles for power that take place between men: it is a disturbing fact that Brutus and Cassius, who had been quarrelling between themselves, make their truce over Portia's dead body, or its representation. Didn't Luce Irigaray argue that the figure of a woman is necessary as the foundation for the pacts of men?[6] Plutarch knew of two different explanations for the death of Portia: he argued in favour of the story that she had killed herself because she was ill and no one would help her. But Shakespeare chooses the other version, the one rejected by Plutarch: 'she, determining to kill herself (her parents and friends carefully looking to keep her from it), took hot burning coals and cast them into her mouth, and kept her mouth so close that she choked herself (*JC* 183). This story takes us into a hideous world, one of mutilation and of fury at psychological abandonment: yet in its image of a mouth closed at all costs in the midst of friends, it picks up resonance. It recalls the silencing and self-destruction that we have seen Portia impose on herself in the name of loyalty and love.

We meet Calpurnia as a woman with a voice and a will of her own for the first time at 2.2. She is only too aware of the dangers by which the life of her husband, Caesar, is threatened in the world outside. Portia knew that something was troubling her husband, whatever he said to the contrary. Both women bring into the world of the play knowledge that is unwelcome, knowledge that has been acquired by accurate observation on their part. But where Portia succeeded in persuading Brutus to confide his plans to her, Calpurnia will not be able to get Caesar to make use of what she knows. Calpurnia has picked up what they intend to do to her husband. Even before she comes in, Caesar is repeating the words that she cried out beside him during the night in her dream: 'Help ho, they murder Caesar!' (2.2.3). Like Portia, Caesar can't help registering something of the disturbance in his partner, though it is made easier for him in that Calpurnia has words and images too, as we find later, for what she fears. Does Calpurnia communicate so vividly because she has never had her mind trained to think like a man, because she lacks Portia's familiarity with philosophy? Caesar doesn't ask Calpurnia what she thinks her dream means, although it is such a specific warning, unlike the generalized threat they both perceived in the thunder and lightning. Caesar never treats Calpurnia's dream as a form of perception or as an opinion that she is offering about the world, maybe because the dream is produced not out of a book but out of her own woman's body, like her voice.

Freud suggested that in nineteenth-century Europe dreams carried knowledge and desires that it was not permissible to admit to in everyday life. It would not be particularly surprising, in view of what we have already seen on the occasion of the Lupercalia, if Calpurnia had some desire of her own to see Caesar dead. I've never heard that giving a wife instructions brings out the best in her. When Caesar turned his back on the Soothsayer in public it was to dismiss him as a dreamer. Unofficial knowledge, the sort that is not sponsored by the state but carried on the individual voice, is easy to dismiss in Rome. Didn't the wife of Pontius Pilate, the Roman governor of Judaea, who warned him not to join in the plot against Jesus, find this out for herself? She sent messages to her husband as he sat in court saying that she had 'suffered many things in a dream because of this just man'. Before the scene is out we may feel that Caesar himself is just a man, merely human, and that like Jesus he too is a victim of collusion among men who are jockeying for power.

With its emphasis on shutting down language, the Roman state wants to outlaw the ability to dream. Today doctors tell us that is not a healthy sign – our bodies need to go every night into that deep sleep where dreaming occurs. Whether we choose to remember our dreams or not is a different question. In private, as we see here, Caesar can't resist a dream, as Cassius told us in the previous scene but it marks a change in him:

> For he is superstitious grown of late,
> Quite from the main opinion he held once
> Of fantasy, of dreams, and ceremonies.

(2.1.195–7)

At the end of his life, according to Jasper Griffin, Caesar felt a sense of futility (HWC 18). Turning to dreams and omens might well be read as a search for a meaning that has been lost, a turn that is made when experience or even life itself has lost its meaning. No one would say that Rome had ever shown much respect for human life, whatever honours it chose to heap on exceptional men. Is the Caesar that Shakespeare invites us to observe exposed in his nightgown here, one who has been left with nothing to believe in, not even much sense of reality, by his unchallenged supremacy in Rome?

Instead of asking Calpurnia about what she dreamed, Caesar sends to the priests. What does he tell them to do but cut up a body (2.2.5), just as Portia cut into herself in search of the truth? Do all Romans suspect that the body holds a secret for them that they have missed? Many of them seem to feel that the body is meant to speak but they don't trust the mouth somehow, it doesn't do the job that it should: 'Speak hands for me!' says Casca (3.1.76). According to Antony, Caesar's wounds 'like dumb mouths do ope their ruby lips' (3.1.260; see also 3.2.215). But Calpurnia, having escaped their education, does not share their secret doubts about language: she is determined to take her dream seriously and to keep her husband at home, a resolve that makes her pit her will against his. 'What mean you, Caesar, think you to walk forth?/You shall not stir out of your house today.' (2.2.8–9). That's a strong statement to make to the man who had taken to himself the title of Dictator for life. How strangely she is answered though, 'Caesar shall forth', her husband says, speaking of himself in the third person, as if he were a monument or an institution rather than a man (2.2.10). He is given to wishful thinking too, for he seems to believe that he can frighten away any threat. But Caesar listens to the priests and that may have confused him, unlike Calpurnia, who has never had any time for their doings – 'never stood on ceremonies', as she puts it herself (2.2.13). It is because Caesar only pays attention to the voices of other men that he will defy Calpurnia's common sense and venture outside.

The priests like to designate frightening experiences as signs: that's one way of playing upon our realistic sense that as human beings we can be hurt. That instinct might at last be attempting to surface in Caesar. But we may also be frightened by our own intimations of power. If Calpurnia takes the storm for a warning sign now, is it because the storm resonates with her own suppressed impulses of violence, a suppressed violence against Caesar that she has also picked up in the other men who surround him and come to her house? As Plutarch said, it only creates trouble for everyone making one man so special.

5

What Calpurnia Knows

There seems to be a general impression, one that I shared myself until I began to pay more careful attention to what Shakespeare wrote, that Calpurnia is almost like a Cassandra, a voice of demented prophecy, an embarrassing figure. Kindest to overlook both of them, never mind if what they claim about what is coming turns out to be accurate. But Cassandra, so the story goes, received her gift of clear vision and her power to articulate it from Apollo and she was being punished by him when she was not believed. Let's see if we can decline to comply with that ancient curse, a curse that might remind us of the sterile curse that Caesar spoke of as he told the silent Calpurnia where to stand. Let's start treating Calpurnia as if she were an ordinary woman, with both her feet on the ground. There's every reason to do so, for she makes no claim that her experience is exceptional. On the contrary, Calpurnia presents herself as one whose experience is shared with other people, others whose voices she carries on her own, rather as Shakespeare himself was telling this very story by means of drama, using many voices.

> There is one within,
> Besides the things that we have heard and seen,
> Recounts most horrid sights seen by the watch.

(2.2.14–16)

'Remember what we heard and saw together during the storm last night?', she asks Caesar. 'Well, there's someone inside, one of the servants, who says that the police who were on duty saw things going on in the streets that would make your hair stand on end.' Of course, Calpurnia doesn't say 'police' but she doesn't use a Roman term either, she speaks of 'the watch'. Shakespeare makes her use the language of his first audience as a way of reminding them that this is not only a story about the past, it is about the present that they are inhabiting too. Readers who think of his reminders of the world of clocks and hats and the watch as lovable slips of the pen, failures of creative imagination on Shakespeare's part, are underestimating him as an artist, or perhaps trying to keep his vision firmly tied to the world that he lived in and apart from the one in which they are living themselves.

The men who make up the watch in *Much Ado About Nothing*, Dogberry and Verges, may not be heroes, any more than the carpenters and cobblers in this Roman play, though they do all have a way with words, but the men of the watch are the ones who have an ear for the truth. In *Much Ado* the conspiracy against Hero is foiled only because of their evidence, when they report what they heard passing in the night. If there has been a conspiracy amongst critics to discredit Calpurnia, one in which we ourselves may unwittingly have joined, it is hard to see how it can survive registering this fact: when Calpurnia talks of lions and of the walking dead, she is repeating what the constables who were guarding the city said they saw, amplifying the voices of servants and of other uneducated people. If some readers think that this makes what she says unreliable, that is not a position which Shakespeare gave evidence of sharing in his plays.

Let's run through that police report for ourselves before we go any further. It's worth a lot of attention, for Shakespeare was fabricating every word of it himself. Plutarch offers only the most general indications of strange goings-on: all the specificity of these images comes from Shakespeare, from the imagination that had been engaged in generating the stage pictures and the language of this play.

> A lioness hath whelpèd in the streets,
> And graves have yawned and yielded up their dead;
> Fierce fiery warriors fight upon the clouds
> In ranks and squadrons and right form of war,
> Which drizzled blood upon the Capitol;
> The noise of battle hurtled in the air,
> Horses did neigh and dying men did groan,
> And ghosts did shriek and squeal about the streets.
>
> (2.2.16–24)

There is an apparently parallel speech in *Richard II*, at 2.4.8, one that tells of the signs of ruin under his rule, which begins 'The bay-trees in our country are all wither'd.' 'How does that speech make you feel?', I once asked a student. 'Frightened', she replied at first, though she came to amend that response. The speech from *Richard* is designed to list signs that indicate impending disaster to the ears of one who believes that the whole natural world is a reflection of the political system. It speaks, as the history plays do, from a position of orthodoxy. But the report of wonders that is made in *Julius Caesar* seems to be different. For one thing, it is designed with reference to the world and the civilization of Rome and it occurs in a play that is not necessarily setting out to endorse that civilization. Why these images, let us ask ourselves, why from this speaker, why now at this point in the play?

When it is too dangerous to express outrage or to speak one's mind, as psychoanalysts tell us, instead people project what remains suppressed in their heads, imagining that they see it in the world outside. The effect is sometimes known as the return of the repressed. The visions that Shakespeare attributes to the watch, the visions that are now voiced by the patrician woman Calpurnia, may tell us something about what both of these parties really think. Suppose Calpurnia picks up and repeats what she has heard in the kitchen because it holds meaning for her too. Shakespeare might even feel that there's some sense in it himself, for after all he is the one who has chosen the images that make up these visions. We ourselves as audience have stood witness as both parties, women and workmen, have been actively silenced and dominated by patrician men. Are we now about to discover that these groups who have not been allowed a voice in public affairs do not share the official beliefs, beliefs supposed to be universally held in Rome?

The visions of the night as reported by the constables on duty are like dreams, dreams of an alternative order or a subversive commentary on the present one. They have a different take on the life that is found in the city, one at variance with the admiring account of Roman civilization that we have inherited in Britain. One of the stories that we still tell about the founding of Roman civilization concerns the she-wolf that suckled Romulus and Remus. Yet for the working men of the watch and for Calpurnia and the women humiliated in the Lupercalia on whose behalf she speaks, it is not a wolf but a lioness that represents the mothers of Rome. These voices offer a challenge to the patrician men who would still be resisting attempts to outlaw the Lupercalia, five hundred years and more after Caesar's death, and only a century before St Augustine set off from Rome to convert England.

'A lioness hath whelpèd in the streets': there can be no more nonsense about the offspring being a different species from the mother when the birth has taken place in public. With this image the lie at the foundation of Rome is exposed, the lie about mothers on which its order has been based. And in a reflex movement the way opens for the truth about Roman order to emerge: as the vision puts it, the graves yawn and are yielding up their dead. Like the lioness, human mothers will fight to the death for their young: but what about fathers, the Roman fathers who bring up their sons to die in battle? What about 'The Old Lie', as Wilfred Owen named it at the time of the First World War, the old lie 'Dulce et decorum est pro patria mori?'[1]

'And graves have yawned and yielded up their dead': let us agree that the images that make up this vision sound like the manifestations of psychosis, but that is only what we might expect to find projected when the symbolic system in which we have been formed ourselves is under challenge: as hearers we feel our own internal sense of order is under attack. If there is psychosis in *Julius Caesar* it is one that is shared by a whole society, one that has been passed down to us, carried on the classical heritage into the present. But these challenging images, this alternative vision, share a logic that can be read. What is more dead to the body and its realities than the patrician men like Brutus and Caesar that we have been meeting in this play? These are the men who have made the rules, the rules that among other things insist on keeping the city in a state that they call 'pure'. They forbid troops to be brought into the city, except on the occasion of a triumph, seeking to keep armed conflict well away from the streets of Rome. Yet conquest by military force is the very pulse by which Roman order lives and extends itself. Fifty battles and more than a million fatalities are what Caesar personally claimed. Suppose all that violence, all those scenes of carnage, were to be admitted to the streets of the city which depends for its wealth on the spoils of conquest? The

Capitol would then be palpably defiled by the blood shed in the name of Rome. The fiery warriors would not be able to keep their heads in the clouds any more. When the men of the watch could hear the sounds of battle in the air and pick up the inarticulate cries of the dying, they were doing no more than acknowledging the central place given to violence in the life of Rome. This violence is associated with the death of language, when only neighing and groaning can be heard. As for those ghosts, with their inarticulate terror, their squealing and shrieking in the streets, surely they couldn't be Roman men giving expression for once to their fear?

Patrician men can command a cast when they want to stage their common fantasies, the ones that organize the way that they live their lives: the Lupercalia, to which our attention has been drawn is one such performance. Who better than Calpurnia – the wife of Caesar, the woman who accepted her submissive part, as we saw, in public – to carry the voice of rebellion and critique? If Shakespeare had given any one individual visions of such hallucinatory power and they had communicated them to the audience directly, there is no doubt that we should have recoiled instinctively, sensing that the speaker was dangerously disturbed. Ophelia and her flowers are quite frightening enough. Instead Shakespeare offers these visions in a highly mediated form, where we are not intended to receive them as the voice of individual madness.

Why this woman, why these images, why now, were the questions that I started by asking. Shakespeare chooses to enter the world of Rome at the moment when it is poised for explosion and disintegration, when the very system intended to protect its life, the assignation of authority to elite men, itself turns out to be the seedbed of violence. Calpurnia, as Caesar's wife, is as close as can be to the focus where that violence is on the point of being unleashed. That may explain why she is suddenly so easy to frighten, so open and resonant to the images of danger that she meets. Calpurnia never cared about signs and portents, 'never stood on ceremonies' before, as she puts it herself in a wording that reminds the audience to compare religion in Rome with religion in Elizabeth's England. It is strange the way the sense of that phrase has been changed.

As we have inherited it today, Calpurnia's meaning has been leached away and a quite different one substituted – 'no need to be so scrupulous, so polite' – almost as if her original statement about herself had been censored out. There were of course Censors in Rome: that is where we get the term from. Part of their job was to keep the wrong sort of person out of the Senate. Perhaps it is only a coincidence that Calpurnia's original meaning, which was also Shakespeare's one, has not made it through into the present. As the wrong sort of attitude, Calpurnia's indifference to the threats identified by the priests has simply not been accorded a public hearing.

Caesar certainly didn't make any response when Calpurnia told him what the watch had seen. 'What can be avoided/ Whose end is purposed by the mighty gods?' (2.2.26–7) is a mere platitude, a step on the way to repeating what he said before Calpurnia spoke, a way of reasserting his own fixed intention. As a wife, Calpurnia may be used to this dynamic recurring when she tries to give a fresh slant to her husband's experience. She gives up on the language of vision and resorts to the language that Caesar hears most easily, the language of flattery. When Calpurnia tells her husband that 'The heavens them-selves blaze forth the death of princes.' (2.2.31), she does it in the knowledge that he enjoys the image of himself as a great world figure, a mover and shaker as we might now say, and so he will hear her and may yet save himself. With that word 'prince', Shakespeare is signalling again to his first audience, asking them to think about the world of contemporary statesmanship, with its strategies for manipulating subjects by means of the mystique of power that had been analysed by Machiavelli in his treatise *The Prince*.

Saving Caesar, her ageing husband, from the effects of his own dissociation, from his own difficulty in admitting to fear and from the inevitable blindness that ensues is the focus of all Calpurnia's energy in this scene. As he approaches 60 and a wife sees time begin to leave its mark upon her husband, she is moved. Caesar was getting on for 60 when he was killed. Does Calpurnia listen with tenderness to Caesar as he struggles to confront the possibility of fear and to name it as his own? 'It seems to me most strange that men should fear' (2.2.35) he says, rather like Mrs Gradgrind, who cannot feel her own death pangs. Dickens made her say 'I think there's a pain somewhere in the room ... but I couldn't positively say that I have got it'.[2] As a city and as a civilization, Rome is filled with fear; the state runs on it, fear is systemic there, as the play has been teaching us. But if any man should name it as his own, at this moment on the morning of 15 March, the day against which the Soothsayer warned him, it is Gaius Julius Caesar.

What is fear but the instinct of self-preservation? If we heard the stirrings of any such instinct in Caesar, he blocked them when he was given the augurers' report:

> The gods do this in shame of cowardice.
> Caesar should be a beast without a heart
> If he should stay at home today for fear.
> No, Caesar shall not. Danger knows full well
> That Caesar is more dangerous than he:
> We are two lions littered in one day,
> And I the elder and more terrible.

(2.2.41–7)

The gods, that is the fiction of masculinity which is worshipped locally, do not permit fear. The omen, true to its disciplinary function, triggers in Caesar an immediate response of submission to this law, even though the absence of a heart in the victim could have been interpreted in various ways. Even so, at the very moment when he boasts of his fearlessness, his ability to destroy before he is destroyed, we hear the muffled voice of another Caesar, one who has felt the resonance of Calpurnia's words and is echoing them, however faintly. He allows himself to utter the word 'danger' and by this moment of realism something is changed for him. When he speaks of himself as 'littered' by a lion-hearted mother, we may be hearing the last gasp of truth from his mouth.

I sometimes think that the historical Caesar stands comparison with Oscar Wilde. Both men saw unflinchingly into their own societies in a way that made them sceptical about the beliefs professed by the educated class into which each of them was born: both became writers. Both were famed for their erotic adventurousness: it is not always remembered now that Caesar was notorious for his sexual exploits with both women and men. But Wilde was an artist and his sceptical clarity was turned to account in works of art. The insight Caesar brought as a young man into the weaknesses of the Roman state were used by him, as other less remarkable men used their own intelligence, to gain power and to take over the state. The Romans were famous engineers: like a good engineer Caesar could not bear to stand by and see work done inefficiently, especially the work of government. Once he had gained absolute power he had used it 'to re-establish order, to restore the economic situation, to extend the franchise of the provincials, to regulate taxation and to reform the calendar' (HWC 18). He seems to have had a livelier sense of the rights and needs of the ordinary people, the plebeians, to have been closer to them than most Romans from patrician families. This made Caesar unpopular and suspect with his own class. He was planning to codify the law and to establish a public library for the people of Rome when he was killed.

At the moment when Shakespeare presents Julius Caesar, at the end of his life, the price that he has paid for his total integration into the Roman state as its supreme icon is being spelled out. He is losing his faculties and the sense that made him human, almost turning into a statue or an automaton. That word may sound a bit modern but in fact it is one that was used by the Greek philosopher Aristotle and it has been borrowed from him in our own day by Jacques Lacan. In Lacan, *automaton* stands for 'the insistence of the signs'.[3] Caesar's behaviour seems to be entirely controlled from outside: he is worked, manipulated like a puppet by impersonal signals. Caesar may well have been walled up away from the experience of the real and trapped in the sign system where he has been made to play such a crucial role. There is something frantic about the way that he turns to random events to find meaning, under the pressure of finding himself made an icon: Caesar was 'superstitious grown of late' (2.1.195). Cassius and other men of his background in the play are quite sceptical about the religious omens and dreams that Caesar turns to now. Calpurnia once knew a different, clear-headed Caesar; 'Alas, my lord,/Your wisdom is consumed in confidence.' (2.2.48–9), she retorts forcefully, while he is still parroting in demented and grandiose fashion 'Caesar shall go forth' (2.2.48). Is the unfortunate man nothing but a disembodied will? But, like Portia, all Calpurnia wants at this point is to minister to her husband as she sees him in jeopardy. What is different in this case though is that Shakespeare lets us see Calpurnia challenge her husband's plan rather than identifying with him and accepting it as Portia did. Though she is arguing with Caesar here, Calpurnia does not desert him but resolutely takes up her own stand by his side. 'Say it's me,' she says, 'say I'm the one who's afraid. Listen, this is what we can do, this is how we will face this crisis together.' And, like Portia, Calpurnia goes down upon her knees.

We do not have to accept that Shakespeare intends to imply that either Caesar or Brutus enjoyed the spectacle of their wives in voluntary abasement. Giving way quickly at such a sight could well mark their own discomfort. People who are not complete monsters are usually made uncomfortable by being treated as if they are more than human and Shakespeare has shown us nothing monstrous about these two men. Bending the knee, like bowing the head or keeping silence, is a sign of submission that some people use in church or in the presence of royalty even today. It could be that something healthy revolts in Caesar and in Brutus too at the sight of their own wives going down on their knees to them at home; it could be that doing that is the last card that these wives who know their husbands so well can play. But the tiny domestic triumph of Calpurnia, where she wins by kneeling, survives only for a breath. Decius comes in before Caesar has finished speaking and once a second Roman man is present the voice of a wife loses any authority it might once have had.

Not for the audience though; we can hear the difference between the urgent clarity of Calpurnia's voice and the empty bonhomie of Decius. It is the voice of Calpurnia's human concern to protect her husband that tunes us, gives us the pitch of honesty, as we listen to the ensuing conversation between men, both of whom are trying to hide what they really want from each other. Decius wants to get Caesar to the Senate in order that he may be attacked: Caesar has registered that his wife believes that it would be wiser to stay at home. 'Say he is sick' (2.2.64), she cuts in, interrupting their conversation, or supplementing it, unable to be silent, afraid that her husband will forget the lines that she has fed him. True enough, Caesar does not sound quite normal, as an audience that has observed his confusion reflectively might agree. But an admission of weakness is not acceptable currency between men and Calpurnia's husband falls back upon the assertion of his will, which is at least something that other men can admire. In doing this, as we might expect, in cutting himself off from all reality, including the reality of his own response, Caesar opens the way to further confusion and this time it is catastrophic. The voice of Calpurnia continues to be part of the scene, but it is carried now by her husband as he recounts her dream, which we hear now in full for the first time. How careful Shakespeare has been to keep any original voicing of prophecy in images that suggested uncanny knowledge out of the mouth of Calpurnia herself. She has always been restricted to reporting the visions of others, while her own is given voice by Caesar himself. Did Shakespeare anticipate how easy it would be for audiences to write off a woman's vision? He seems to have gone out of his way to prevent that from happening. It is Caesar who tells us of what Calpurnia knows. How could her dream acquire greater authority for us than that?

Don't let's pretend that we don't ourselves share in the feelings of these Romans. In spite of ourselves, in spite of all our gestures of sceptical dissent, something in us wants to believe in Caesar. We also want to see him die. We're all sitting there waiting for him to be killed; that's what we've come to see. If there is any compunction in us, any tension between wanting to see Caesar die and pity for him it has been nurtured in us by the efforts of Calpurnia on his behalf. The Caesar we have just been watching is like the parody of a man. Calpurnia knows even this and still she wants to save him, as her husband, deaf to the implications of her fantasy, now reports.

> She dreamt tonight she saw my statue,
> Which like a fountain with an hundred spouts
> Did run pure blood, and many lusty Romans
> Came smiling and did bathe their hands in it.

(2.2.76–9)

At last we hear it, the dream or should we say the nightmare of Caesar's wife. How would a friend or a therapist read it today? Hundreds of Romans, his wife, the conspirators, this audience, would have some reason to take satisfaction in seeing the death that is about to take place. The act that will show that Caesar is no more than an ordinary man with a vulnerable body will restore a sense of sanity to the stage. Or will it? What is sanity? What are we saying? 'Who would have thought the old man to have had so much blood in him?' mourned a woman who underestimated her own instinctive recoil from the shedding of blood.

Perhaps we should try to read that dream not just as a wish for revenge but as a diagnosis. Or better still maybe as a work of art. We might start by reminding ourselves to look at the illustrations in medieval manuscripts if we want to see the fountain Calpurnia's imagination painted, one that was a solid structure of metal or stone, housing pipes for dispensing water from a natural source. The leaping fountains of baroque Rome were still far in the future. Fountain structures were set up in towns and cities in Shakespeare's day to provide a water supply for the community. In the city of Cambridge, you can still find the decorated stone structure that was called 'The Fountain' when it was put up in Cambridge market place in 1614 (see plate 5). This Fountain was a public utility, but religious communities too, as architectural historians tell us, built such fountains in their cloisters for common use, for drawing water and for washing hands: The Fountain put up in 1600, around the time that this play was written, still stands in the Great Court of Trinity College in the university.

If Calpurnia has seen Caesar turned into an object, something not human, which is unable to perceive or feel and cannot speak, that is not far from what we have seen of him ourselves. We too have begun to suspect that Caesar is less like a full-blooded man than he should be and that the place which he fills in the city serves interests that are not necessarily his own. In the midst of her dream, Calpurnia cried aloud 'Help ho, they murder Caesar!': as audience we are fully expecting to see Caesar's body in death, stuck with metal shafts, like the structure of the fountain Calpurnia saw. Calpurnia's vision encompasses this future attack, but it goes further: it teaches us to recognize a spiritual reality underlying that material form, underlying the shape that the conspirators' attack will take. The woman whose voice is silenced in public – even now it is her husband who reports her words – has made her own analysis of the bloodthirsty culture of Rome. She sees the price that her husband pays for the place he has won in it and she names the dissociation that is imposed on all these men who must learn to

Plate 5 'The Fountain'

This structure, now removed to the corner of Lensfield Road,
Cambridge, was called 'The Fountain' in 1614 when it was set up to
provide a common water supply in Cambridge market-place. A spout,
now replaced by a stone chock, stood at each of its six faces.

smile as they bathe in blood.

Fear and horror are a wife's response to this knowledge, a recoil that we are invited to share as the symbols she has made in her dream reverberate in us. But Calpurnia seems to be talking about religion too: there is something almost pious about the attitude of the Romans with their handwashing in her dream. Pontius Pilate was a Roman who was famous for washing his hands. 'I am innocent of the blood of this just man', he proclaimed at the trial of Jesus. Does Shakespeare link the image of these Romans, who smilingly accept the murder of Caesar, with the learned men who might wash their hands at the fountain in their cloister? It would be a pity to miss the hint that Shakespeare was giving to his first audience, for whom the word 'fountain' was closely associated with the church and with Christian symbolism, as the *OED* reports. The term fountain was used also of the font where baptisms took place, while in the Prayer Book God was addressed as 'the fountain of all wisdom'. In the language of redemption, the faithful were called to bathe in the blood of Christ. By means of her dream, Calpurnia asks the audience to think about a fountain that does not produce wisdom but violence and dissociation, one that invites a loss both of humanity and of common sense.

'*New Presbyter* is but *Old Priest* writ Large', wrote the poet Milton.[4] He was writing forty years after Shakespeare's death but he seems to be addressing a problem which had not gone away in the interim. Like Calpurnia, Milton also had a dream: according to Milton's worst nightmare the reformation of Christianity would not make any difference, the underlying evils and abuses of the Roman church would survive. Among them the overweening authority of the priests was foremost, because in Milton's terms it overruled individual conscience; that is, it paid no respect to ordinary people's intelligence or to their understanding, the faculties that Shakespeare's own work as an artist was trying to call into play. Interpreting the scriptures, for instance, was reserved for the authority of priests. Decius in *Julius Caesar* may not be a priest but he certainly sounds like one. He takes over Calpurnia's dream, ignoring the fact that it made her scream out in her sleep, and proceeds to torture the image into a meaning of his own, a meaning that we as audience know he is fabricating in order to gain control over Caesar's behaviour.

The mind, no less than the body, is ruined by torture, as Elaine Scarry has shown in her book *The Body in Pain*.[5] When Decius urges Caesar and Calpurnia, who is standing by mutely, to experience her dream as a good one, is he offering a violation to their intelligence? Perhaps both things could be happening; he might be adding insult to injury as we say. His act of interpretation will open the way to Caesar's death, it is true, but he does it by first destroying the defences created for them both by Calpurnia's mind, by wiping out what she has understood about Rome and exposed.

> This dream is all amiss interpreted,
> It was a vision fair and fortunate.
> Your statue spouting blood in many pipes,
> In which so many smiling Romans bathed,
> Signifies that from you great Rome shall suck
> Reviving blood and that great men shall press
> For tinctures, stains, relics, and cognisance.
> This by Calpurnia's dream is signified.

(2.2.83–9)

Decius may take in Caesar but he is not fooling us: 'spouting' Shakespeare makes him say, a term that was already associated with a glib sort of fluency. That may be a reminder to pay attention to the way Decius himself speaks. Shakespeare seems to be drawing very closely on Christian vocabulary and imagery for the language of Decius, even while he frames them so that they are associated with lying and manipulation. What sucked blood, for his first audience, but verminous creatures like bedbugs or possibly leeches in the name of making sick people better? Seeing, in her fantasy, Romans steep their hands in her husband's blood was enough to make Calpurnia scream and to disgust us in the audience when we heard it described but the Roman Decius lets us know that there could be a greater horror even than shedding blood, when he himself makes bloodshed into something holy. You rarely hear that the audience faints at *Julius Caesar*, although they're expected to do so at *King Lear*: the St John's Ambulance crews stand ready in the foyer. I saw people leave Deborah Warner's *Titus Andronicus* before it was over too. Perhaps audiences find it easy to defend themselves against the imagery of *Julius Caesar* because it's already familiar

55

to them from Christianity. They've been taught not to recoil from the image of drinking the blood of Christ.

There seems to be a desperate longing for intimacy in Rome, even if it is distorted in the forms it takes. When Decius speaks of Caesar's blood as reviving, and of its being sucked, he is not drawing on any tradition from ancient Rome but he is recognizably echoing imagery used closer to Shakespeare's time, the imagery of traditional English Christianity. The work of Caroline Walker Bynum has shown us that some holy women in the medieval period claimed to be nourished by nursing on the blood of Christ.[6] It was 'a desire for the most intimate possible contact with the body of the dead saint', in the words of Katharine Park, that seemed to underlie the attempt to obtain relics of them, relics that might take the form of a cloth that had been dipped in their blood.[7] Even water in which a bone of the saint had been steeped might contain a tincture of them. At this present moment in history, when once again the faithful are petitioning the Pope to upgrade the status of Mary the mother of Jesus, I ask myself about this drive for intimate contact with what was holy. Was the cult of relics an attempt to re-establish the mother and her body at the centre of sacred experience – an instinctive resistance to the way the importance of mothers is diminished and obscured under patriarchal rule? Christian rituals, as we have seen, are close to Roman ones in the way that they deal with mothers.

'This by Calpurnia's dream is signified' (2.2.90), Decius insists. From the first moment of this play the Romans have been trying to take command of signification. What meaning is the body to carry for the people of Rome? There is a sense in which the body itself is the source of all meaning, as André Green has argued, for it is only by the affects, the body's pulse of response to experience, that we are connected as human creatures to the world about us.[8] The interpretation imposed by Decius makes use of language to put the affects of Calpurnia into reverse. He systematically misrepresents what Calpurnia is saying through the image in her dream.

Decius may sound like a Christian priest but by rank he is a patrician and for him, as for other privileged Romans, nothing was holier than his ancestors. When Decius speaks of 'stains' and 'relics', he groups them together with 'tinctures' and 'cognisances', terms which have been associated with heraldry, the science which draws up pedigrees, where descent is traced from father to son. Decius seems to be mapping out a future use for the blood of Caesar, to be handed down as relics were within families, handed down from the past: a tradition that will continue to validate authority as it is passed down between privileged men. An art that is involved in deception may come into this process of transmission, too, for 'tincture' was a word associated with cosmetics and 'stain' with adding colour, as in painting. Later editors of Shakespeare, even Samuel Johnson have seemed to find it difficult to grasp the dramatist's point here: Johnson said that he found this speech 'somewhat confused' (JC 90). Isn't it the reader, Johnson, who has the problem, when he balks at moving as nimbly as the logic of poetry can move? Johnson was reflecting on Shakespeare during Britain's Augustan age, a time when admiration for the classical tradition as established by the emperor Augustus was being renewed. We know that Johnson also clung to his Christian faith. It might have something to do with his fervent belief in monarchy too. Isn't Johnson famous for answering that it was not for him to bandy compliments with his sovereign, when he was asked what he'd replied to the king's kind remarks about the *Dictionary* he had composed? In order to read the play that Shakespeare wrote at the turn of the seventeenth century, a hundred and fifty years before Johnson was born, do we have to be prepared, as Shakespeare was, to question every tradition, political or religious, that came down from Rome? Maybe we have to be prepared to listen like him to the voices of women, whether they are speaking from the position of critics or just putting into words what they know about their own husbands.

6

Roman Men

It is not surprising that the leading men of Rome want to kill
Caesar. It seemed pretty obvious to Plutarch at least: 'For, men
striving who should most honour him, they made him hateful
and troublesome to themselves that most favoured him, by
reason of the unmeasurable greatness and honours which they
gave him', he wrote (*JC* 155). If we want to discover whether
Shakespeare was in agreement with Plutarch, let us pause to
consider the actions that lead to that moment when Caesar
leaves the safety of his home for the Capitol. The difference
between women and men, the supreme difference, as inheritors
of the Roman tradition may still like to think of it, might turn out
to be less cardinal than the differences, the constant competitive
thrusting, that continually arises between men. Now that we've
seen both murderer and victim, Brutus and Caesar, as vulnerable
and as husbands, we may be better placed to understand the
process that will put them at different ends of the knife. The
tensions between them, which arise because they are both
powerful educated men, are alone responsible for this polarization, for the Roman crowd sees plenty to love in each of them.
Like his close friend, Caesar, Brutus 'sits high in all the people's
hearts' (1.3.157).

At the opening of the play, the crowd seemed full of
intelligence, full of high spirits and good will. It is only later,
in the wake of the violent acts of their so-called superiors, the
conspirators, that they too break out into violence themselves,
destroying property, interrogating and then killing the poet
Cinna. It is as if violence, a violence implicit in the suppression
of their language, were an infection that the tribunes had passed
on to them. And of course, they were only doing the kind of
thing that Roman armies were supposed to do, strictly outside

58

Rome. But the crowd never lose their enthusiasm for Caesar, the pleasure they take in him as a man, that brings them bounding onto the stage as the first scene opens. These people are looking for someone they can respect, someone whom they can also recognize as like themselves; that is why they are ready to put up a statue of Brutus so soon after he has helped to kill Caesar (3.2.42). Editors do not always appreciate that this is a sign of other things besides fickleness in the crowd: the impulse to honour something they can recognize as human like themselves is vital in them. It springs out of the deep sources of their life.

But respect depends on its corollary, self-respect, and these can be a problem for a leading man in Rome, as the figure of Cassius, the man who sets up the plot to kill Caesar, reveals to us. He can't bear that a man so like himself as Caesar should have such unique standing; it makes Cassius himself feel diminished. Maybe he doesn't like being reminded of how it felt to be a child, either:

> Why, man, he doth bestride the narrow world
> Like a Colossus, and we petty men
> Walk under his huge legs and peep about
> To find ourselves dishonourable graves.
>
> (1.2.135–8)

As Caesar, who does understand other men, tells us in passing, Cassius is full of contempt for the impulses of his own spirit.

> Seldom he smiles, and smiles in such a sort
> As if he mocked himself and scorned his spirit
> That could be moved to smile at any thing.
>
> (1.2.205–7)

Dangerous, very dangerous, this state of radical self-hatred, this alienation, repeats Shakespeare through the voice of Caesar, the man who knows about men but is trapped in Rome.

The story of Roman marriage is bound in, according to the logic of Shakespeare's imagination, with the story of Roman treachery and betrayal between men. The alienation from women and from their own inner lives that he has marked in showing how Roman men live within marriage, Shakespeare will track as it destroys the life of the community and its peace. I've heard it said that there is no way to define peace, yet as I work on this play I have come to wonder whether that is true.

The word peace might be a way of naming the freedom to live out whatever life each of us finds within ourselves. But Roman men seem to be alarmed by the inner life. When he hears a flourish of trumpets, Brutus starts and is even ready to admit to fear, a fear that he is quick to associate with a political rather than a personal explanation. 'I do fear the people/Choose Caesar for their king' (1.2.78–9). His problem with language, with naming what is going on inside him, which Shakespeare makes accessible to us through Portia's account, renders Brutus utterly vulnerable to the manipulations of Cassius.

'Intellectual' is a term that psychologists use to describe those people who use thinking to orientate themselves in the world, and to organize their experience. When Brutus says, on his first appearance, 'I am not gamesome' (1.2.28), it could be an admission of depression – at least that is how refusals to throw ourselves in are sometimes pathologized. People who don't join in with enthusiasm are often made to feel unpopular. But there could be another explanation for his behaviour. If Brutus holds back from the celebrations of community life in which Antony takes an untroubled part, the reason might be that by disposition he is not sick but intellectual, in the sense that psychologists use the word. Brutus is experiencing disturbance, as he acknowledges to Portia his wife. What if his distemper is caused by trying to think about life in Rome? It is difficult, as we know, to think outside the terms that the language of one's own culture affords. They limit what can be conceptualized and expressed. The only image that Brutus has for his inner confusion, when he excuses himself to Cassius at 1.2.46, is a battle: 'poor Brutus, with himself at war,/Forgets the shows of love to other men.'; linguistically he is driven back to the bedrock of his militaristic culture. To bring perceptions not endorsed by that culture into consciousness, he would need to find another language, one not made in Rome, as Calpurnia did.

Although defeating an external enemy is cause for honour, the structure of competition which threatens to dominate relations between men inside Rome is never directly named: we see it acted out in the sacred race of the Lupercalia or hear a hint of it in the form of verbal imagery that plays on the distance between high and low, what is elevated and what is debased, but it is never straightforwardly acknowledged. Differences of degree enforced by active subjugation are presumed to raise patrician men over both women of their own rank and the commoners, but these hierarchies are also perpetuated among patrician men. They live in fear of their own subjugation to another man. It might be this which leaves Brutus, the idealistic philosopher, starting with fear at an emotion that he cannot recognize. Is Cassius playing on the wish in Brutus to compete with Caesar, to stop him from winning the one and only crown, a wish that is so strong, perhaps, because it is unnamed? 'Caesar doth bear me hard, but he loves Brutus.' (1.2.302), as Cassius reminds the audience. Surely no rational argument, nothing less than a desire that is powerful but unacknowledged, could make Brutus even think of betraying the man who is known to have taken him into his heart.

The play moves from one conspiracy to another: if the first is carried on between the tribunes, to damp down the signs of popular enthusiasm for Caesar, the second – and there will be more of them – is the plot that is directed against Brutus, the plot to convince him that the best men, the finest minds, the most influential people thought that he should lead a bid to overthrow Caesar. The flattery that will coax Caesar out to meet his death works first on Brutus. At 1.2.297–311 Cassius spells out his intentions like a stage devil in the old morality plays: Shakespeare wants to make sure we don't miss understanding how open these Romans are to manipulation. Cassius involves Casca too before he gives Cinna the task of planting 'evidence' that there is a widespread desire for Brutus to take the lead – to take the lead in an action that Cassius himself has been stage-managing from the start.

Though Cassius does want to get rid of Caesar, he also has tender feelings for him. 'Poor man' (1.3.104), he says, it's not his fault he's in the position he's in, we're the ones who put him there. The need to follow a leader, to trust and believe in someone, seems to have gone wrong in Rome. In case we can't understand how that is playing out in Brutus himself, Shakespeare offers us a pocket guide in the example of Caius Ligarius, the sick man who came on his own to join the conspiracy late. Shakespeare makes him cast off his kerchief onstage, stand there and remove the badge of sickness that he was wearing. What is wrong with Caius Ligarius, or is it rude to ask? Shakespeare, who knows his audience so well, might be counting on our shameless curiosity here. Or perhaps he wants us to notice what Ligarius is doing that is dangerous. Bravado, that is empty gestures, might come into it; throwing off that badge is not going to restore Ligarius to health or make him better, it's not going to touch his underlying problem at all, even though it might impress some people, maybe even critics. How brave and dedicated of Ligarius, they might say, or even, when the going gets tough the tough get going. This admiring response is not one that the play itself invites. Wait for the end of the scene, when Ligarius enthuses:

> with a heart new fired I follow you
> To do I know not what; but it sufficeth
> That Brutus leads me on.

(2.1.331–3)

Immediately the words pass his lips, a growl of thunder in the background, the wordless notation of the playwright, 'listen, mark', refuses to let this blithe abdication of responsibility, this voluntary blindness, pass. When Brutus accepts the terms in which Ligarius frames their relationship, he is agreeing to replicate the old forms, to stand himself in the place of the unquestioned leader. 'Follow me then' (2.1.333), he says, putting an end to any chance of radical change.

As the play reminds us, Brutus has actually been invited to make a repetition of history, to play the part that his own ancestor once played in casting out a tyrant, the name that became associated with kingship, with one man in possession of too much power. But what if they are calling Caesar a tyrant now and wanting to cast him out for reasons that the patricians we are watching in this play don't understand? What if they are blind to the connection between wanting a leader to believe in and coming to hate that leader? Accepting a leader, for Ligarius, seems to mean giving away his own power, the power to think and make judgements for himself; it means choosing obedience. We talk sometimes of systems of belief as tyrannous, isn't that so? Brutus has just revealed to us that he himself is prepared to fill the place of unquestioned leader among a group of Roman men; could they all be trapped together in acting out a system of beliefs that are going unnamed?

The workmen seemed to resist wearing their badges of identification, but Ligarius is more docile and he wears a kerchief to mark the sickness that no killing of Caesar can heal, a kerchief that in Elizabeth's England would more often be found on the head of a young girl. Is it something to do with girls, then, something to do with beliefs about women and girls that needs to be put right in Rome? The distemper might have its counterpart in the England of Elizabeth too, in some disease or distemper in the culture that was not cured in spite of all his efforts when her father Henry VIII cast off the tyranny of Rome.

The voices of girls echo in the heads of the men in Shakespeare's play. These men associate them, oddly enough, with Caesar. 'Every woman's husband and every man's wife', as his soldiers actually described him. But Cassius for one doesn't seem to think much of girls, or the ability to take their place, and he connects both with illness: when Caesar had a fever once in Spain and was so weak with it – trembling, pale and dull-eyed – that he had to be nursed, Cassius noted with distaste and disapproval that his cry for water had sounded like the voice of a sick girl.

> I did hear him groan,
> Ay, and that tongue of his that bade the Romans
> Mark him and write his speeches in their books,
> 'Alas', it cried, 'give me some drink, Titinius',
> As a sick girl.

> (1.2.124–8)

Was it the unwelcome revelation that there was no real difference between a girl and Caesar, that one was as liable to develop a fever as another, the very lesson that Portia was offering to Brutus, which made Cassius so unsympathetic to the sick man?

Cassius seemed to feel that the voices of girls should never have to be heard. He bears a grudge against Caesar even for being ill, just as he was enraged at the memory that he himself had had to save Caesar from drowning. The fiction that Caesar is more than mortal, different from any other human being, is constantly at risk. 'Tis true, this god did shake' (1.2.121), says Cassius scornfully. What makes him so angry as he tells these stories? You could imagine remembering them as touching

63

scenes. Could it be that Cassius has an intuition that the structure of his own identity, his belief in himself and in his right to be listened to with respect as a Roman man is undermined by them? He has to acknowledge that Caesar needs the help of others just to stay alive. It reminds Cassius perhaps that like the rest of us he too had only survived because a woman had once cared for him when he was an infant and helpless, that when he was without speech – as the term *infans,* which means 'lacking speech' in Latin, implies – a woman had taught him language. This may be the historical truth, the truth about their own history that Roman men will do anything to forget.

This is not an incidental point: in case we missed it the first time, Shakespeare repeats it a hundred lines further on, when Casca describes Caesar's attack of epilepsy. This time the notion of mothers and the wish to obliterate them is named. We may have noticed Caesar's frailty for ourselves but we are invited to register how it affects other Roman men. They seem to be made uneasy by the question of sympathy. They don't like to see it asked for or offered.

> And so he fell. When he came to himself again, he said if he had done or said anything amiss, he desired their worships to think it was his infirmity. Three or four wenches where I stood cried, 'Alas, good soul', and forgave him with all their hearts. But there's no heed to be taken of them: if Caesar had stabbed their mothers they would have done no less. (1.2.260)

Of course, the stabbing that we've come to the play to see is the stabbing of Caesar, but Casca turns things round to make out that the girls are the villains. The reminder of a sympathy that the official world of Rome has banished is carried on the voices of these girls: beneath his tough repudiations of such a wish, this may be what a Roman man really longs for. What upset Brutus most of all seemed to be his sense of the active sympathy between Caesar and the crowd, the way that each side appealed and responded to the other.

Something comes between Roman men and the desire of their hearts. Is it language, or the way that they have learned to use it, the way that they have learned to think, living in Rome? As playwright, Shakespeare is not to be identified with any one of the characters that we see staged, but he did control what all of them could say. That might prompt us to listen rather attentively when he chooses to put that very admired Roman master of language, Cicero, the great Roman orator and statesman, as the reference books have it, on the stage. Cicero's speeches and his command of language were legendary. They established the standard for eloquence in public life. Cicero is the man who has been credited with bringing 'Latin prose to its perfection, whereby it became the basis of literary expression in the languages of modern Europe' (OCCL). Leading figures in the Christian intellectual tradition, from the early church fathers to St Augustine and Petrarch, modelled their writing on him: Queen Elizabeth had famously read all his works by the time she was 16. But when Shakespeare brings the man who moulded the forms of language in which the intellectual tradition of Europe was created onto the stage, in the scene where he meets Casca out in the storm, it is to expose an impoverished figure. All Cicero has to offer his hearers is a warning: don't bother trying to understand what's going on around you. You don't want to be wrong.

> Indeed, it is a strange-disposèd time.
> But men may construe things after their fashion
> Clean from the purpose of the things themselves.
>
> (1.3.33–5)

Prim and passive in the face of extreme experience, Cicero the great orator, the manipulator of language, is unable to respond with Casca's emotional generosity or to risk an attempt to understand (see plate 6). He is a warning against the intellectual life in himself. Of course, there might be other ways of making sense than those used in classical prose: the associative logic of the psyche which is mobilized by means of poetry might offer a serious alternative. But Rome, as Shakespeare demonstrates by means of the attack on Cinna, is a city where poets are torn apart in the street. The poet who breaks in on Brutus and Cassius in Act 4 has only moralizing doggerel to offer.

When Cicero discouraged him from interpretation, Casca was describing the signs of a disorder that is supernatural, or it might be more truthful to admit that it is a spiritual one, a disorder afflicting the inner lives of the people, signs that he saw in the streets of the city of Rome. Could it be that Shakespeare

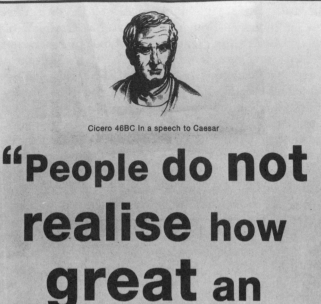

Cicero 46BC In a speech to Caesar

"People do not realise how great an income saving is"

For more information about how to save
as little as £50 per month with M&G either
call us now on (0990) 600631 or write to:
The M&G Group, Bristol BS38 7ET,
or e-mail on hb@MandG.reply.Co.UK

Issued by M&G Securities Ltd (regulated by IMRO and the Personal Investment Authority).
M&G does not offer investment advice or make any recommendations about investments.
We only market the packaged products and services of the M&G marketing group.

M&G

Managing your money for the longer term

Plate 6   Cicero's portrait and one of his sayings

1997 advertisement from the *Guardian* newspaper, where a quotation
from Cicero's writing is used to identify him with a rational approach to
personal gain, in order to recommend a savings plan.

wants us to act on Cicero's hint and ask ourselves about the way that Romans interpret what they see? Has Casca, for instance, been able to read the signs in the skies and the streets? Casca is used to storms in nature, he says; he seems ready enough to interpret those, as he speaks of 'scolding winds', an 'ambitious ocean' and 'threatening clouds' (1.3.5–8). But perhaps he is only revealing his basic frame of reference here, the one which structures his imagination and makes it work, the notion of rivalry and of rebuke. That sounds like the echo of a Roman education, all right, whether it takes place in a public school of today or a religious one. The sights that met him in the streets of his own city Casca cannot explain, except to say that they are 'portentous things/Unto the climate that they point upon'. Casca, Cassius and the other conspirators, some editors of Shakespeare too, would like you to think that these signs point towards Caesar's death, that they are a divine indication that the universe itself would like to see him killed. But we know that the wish to see him dead is a human one and that we share in it ourselves; that is why we are sitting here.

There are none so blind as those who will not see, says the old proverb. What are these patrician men who are the friends of Caesar and his fellow officers in the state refusing to look at, refusing to admit? Is it their own personal desire to punish Caesar for his successes in the field and with the populace and for the authority that they themselves have allowed him to usurp? They were the ones who sat in the Senate and voted him those exceptional titles, those unheard of personal honours. But perhaps there is something just as important that the senators do not dream of seeing, something that meets them every day on the streets of Rome that they have been educated to avoid noticing before.

> never till tonight, never till now,
> Did I go through a tempest dropping fire.
> Either there is a civil strife in heaven,
> Or else the world, too saucy with the gods,
> Incenses them to send destruction.

> (1.3.9–13)

Casca first hazarded that the storm over Rome might be a sign of civil war among the gods, but amended that guess to suggest that the gods might be rebuking the world, as if it were a child who had been too outspoken. If he has already revealed how his experience of education has shaped his own capacity for exploratory thought, now he indicates how it has limited it too. Casca stops short, like a once saucy child who has learned his lesson now. Casca has learned to dissociate. He can name the idea of civil strife but he disconnects it from the real world in which he lives, expels it from the city and will contemplate it only as a possibility among the gods. He even names the gods, a shorthand, as we have already seen in this play, for patrician or patriarchal power. But any idea that the way elite men have seized control of power might be dangerous, that it might be imperilling the safety of the whole city, remains unformulated and unspoken within Casca. It is aborted before it reaches the threshold of speech.

Casca is able to report what he knows only in terms of images that he has witnessed, for which, like dreams, he will be asked to take no responsibility. We are the ones who need to be prepared to interpret what Shakespeare is offering us by means of Casca and through his words. What has he seen in the city but fire, a fire that plays about the figures of men. At the same time, he has seen much that is familiar there: 'A common slave – you know him well by sight –' (1.3.14). If the fire turned the hand of this slave into a flaming sign, according to Casca's report, can we guess what it was a sign of? Something to do with labour perhaps and with the men who work with their hands for a bare living, even as slaves work just for their keep? The angry lion that he saw which forebore from attacking him, could that be a lion who belonged in the city, a lion that was exiled from it when mothers were associated with wolves?

> Against the Capitol I met a lion
> Who glazed upon me and went surly by
> Without annoying me. And there were drawn
> Upon a heap a hundred ghastly women,
> Transformèd with their fear, who swore they saw
> Men, all in fire, walk up and down the streets.

> (1.3.20–5)

The loose and associative logic of this poetry allows connections to be made between the surly lion and the frightened women, between the women's fear and the sight of the men all in fire. We may be moved to remember the young men of the Lupercalia, who went about the streets offering threats. Early in the play as this is, we may guess that this fire may be connected with anger or violence and that the powerful men of Rome, the men who have attempted to control both women and working men, are in danger themselves. We may even suspect where that danger for men lies, now we have seen Casca, the associate of Cicero the statesman and stylist, draw back from complete knowledge and stop short of recognizing the anger and fear in the hearts of many in Rome.

7

The Escape from Delusion

The first half of *Julius Caesar* offers the image of a grand seduction: it tells how Brutus the philosopher is tempted into playing the assassin and how the man of experience, Caesar, is talked into suppressing his intelligence of danger. Words like 'honourable' and 'noble', the official praise language of Rome, as Cassius ironically affirms at 1.2.297–300, are shown to be empty categories and to point in the direction of slaughter. By the time that Brutus plans to run through the market armed with a bloody sword and shouting 'freedom', Shakespeare has taught us to look out for the immeasurable gap between word and substance in the talk of educated men. We might well pause to ask ourselves a question after all this: how does Shakespeare manage to salvage these men for us in spite of what we know about them, how does he make us care what happens after Caesar's death?

Some people might find the quarrel between Brutus and Cassius at 4.3 undignified, or in order to make sense of it seek to work out which of them was in the right. As a critic, I could join in this game and remind you that there were some very unpleasant stories told about Brutus himself and money, stories about starving his Salaminian debtors to death. But as readers, or as Shakespeare's attentive audience, we may have learned to feel reservations about copying the self-justifying and recriminatory style of Rome. Let's observe instead that a different sense of that quarrel can be made if we hear the angry voices of men as the voices of boys, or even as the voices of children; that would not seem inappropriate, for they are tense with the passions of the playground:

> I denied you not.
> You did.
> I did not.

(4.3.82–4)

In many cultures, not only in the culture of Europe, it is insulting to say that a grown man is like a child. As we have seen, the Romans in this play don't like to remember that they were ever helpless themselves. Instead they have created a fantasy of who they are, a fantasy of masculinity that this play has exposed. When Shakespeare makes Brutus and Cassius let down their guard in private, they reveal that underneath the official pose of invulnerability they feel anger and fear, the anger and fear of children who know that they cannot survive in isolation and are terrified that they will be abandoned and betrayed. Once we have been allowed to see them admitting that they are vulnerable and human, how can we withhold our concern from Brutus and his friend? We can begin to love these men now, in spite of the bombast and self-deception in which they arm themselves, and which never quite disappear. And we register a shift as Shakespeare summons the weight of that earlier scene between Brutus and Cassius into play: we feel a managing hand controlling the energies that have been released. That may be what we mean by aesthetic satisfaction here: the intimation, without words or beyond them, that an economy is being brought into balance, that sense is being made.

That is not to claim that a vision of final harmony is offered by this play: *Julius Caesar* suggests if anything that excessive harmony or deference in relationships might be only a dangerous front, and that tension and difference are a part of intimacy. But the play does its best to make sure that confusion on the part of the audience is resolved. There is a satisfying rounding out achieved by Shakespeare's art: when we see Roman warriors act wildly or speak using inflated terms in the last two acts of the play we now understand the code that generates this behaviour. The action may be muddled, but we have been equipped to identify the deep structures that underpin life in Rome. Brutus and Cassius may not extricate themselves from the Roman contempt for mothers. When they make up, it is on his mother – 'that rash humour which my mother gave me' (4.3.120) – that Cassius blames his disposition.

71

But we in the audience now hear that complaint with irony and even with tenderness. If these Romans feel so angry with the women that bore them, if anger informs the action of the play from the start, could that fury be traced to a long-ago moment of shock? Once upon a time these men were abandoned, as it must have seemed to them, by the mothers who had nurtured and protected them as infants, when they were handed over to the fathers of Rome to be made into fighting men.

The bloody coup these men have worked for only confirms Roman order: it is impossible for men whose interior life is disavowed and misnamed by this order to produce change. We watch as the tradition we have learned to view only with horror begins to play itself out over again but this time in permutations that are new. The conspirators thought that they were going to deliver Rome from tyranny for ever, just as the World War of 1914–18 was to be the war to end all wars. (As educated people, we are often reminded that the title of the Czar, who was put to death by his own countrymen in 1918, was derived from 'Caesar', like the title of the Kaiser, who led Germany into that war.) Instead, as we uneasily recognize from our place in the audience during the second half of the play, we have somehow seen all this before and so has Rome. The underlying structures of fantasy that shape the sense of identity in Roman men, as we have seen, take the form of legend and of ritual; these have remained unchallenged and are continuing to exert their ancient force.

Cassius is aware that he is acting out an old story: 'Be thou my witness that against my will/(As Pompey was) am I compelled to set/Upon one battle all our liberties.' (5.1.73–5), he laments. Cassius had once refused to submit to the fear of omens that had usurped the common sense of other men: he was a genuine rebel against the confusion and mystification of Roman life, but he was under an illusion in thinking that he could escape from the tyranny of the system itself, for that had been planted deep inside him. 'Thunder', growled the playwright in dissent when Cassius had once claimed 'That part of tyranny that I do bear/I can shake off at pleasure.' (1.3.99–100). By the end of the play, he is beginning to take notice of omens, as Caesar did. He too is looking for a meaning that has eluded his direct vision. Although he has revealed that what he really feels is despair,

Cassius also mouths the same hollow but compulsive language of defiance: 'For I am fresh of spirit and resolved/To meet all perils very constantly.' (5.1.90–91). Rome takes over his voice at the end as it took over Caesar's.

Brutus the intellectual is never disillusioned: even when haunted by the ghost of the friend he helped to kill, he embodies the confusion of Rome to the end. When we hear that ghost identify himself before Brutus, not as Caesar but as the evil spirit of Brutus himself – 'Thy evil spirit, Brutus' (4.3.282), it replies when questioned – we may sense, as those who have accompanied Brutus through so much, that he is at last confronted in hallucination by that part of himself, those feelings of resentment and hate, that he was unable to recognize and name in words. But there is still no way for him to make that fruitful recognition, one that once given currency in Rome might help to change its ways. No such clarity transpires to enlighten the confusion of Rome: if the later scenes of *Julius Caesar* have always seemed tedious and difficult to follow, that may be because in them repetition and confusion are being openly played out. They are given an elaborate staging in the repeated misunderstandings of the final battle scenes.

Our own disillusion as audience begins with Mark Antony. This man stood before us first as a figure of promise, as the naked body of a vigorous man, before Shakespeare used others to describe him as a man who knew about pleasure and could find it in music and plays. Antony only starts taking up a speaking part after his appearance on the scene of Caesar's murder: here is a new man, we dare to hope, a different kind of Roman. His command of the situation, his readiness with a language that expands and resonates to match our own sense of that moment in all its tragedy, seem to strike a fresh note of hope.

> Live a thousand years,
> I shall not find myself so apt to die:
> No place will please me so, no mean of death,
> As here by Caesar, and by you cut off,
> The choice and master spirits of this age.

> (3.1.159–63)

But what are these phrases? apt to die? choice and master spirits? command? Are we ourselves even now, after all that we have seen of Rome, ready to be seduced by a language that claims that the men who govern, men with blood on their hands, are the choicest natures alive? Once we have noticed this, we may hear the stirring oratory of Antony rather differently, realizing that for all his magnetism, he too is a son of Rome.

The pleasure we cannot help but take in Antony marks out how far we too are accomplices in Rome. His self-possession in the moment of crisis when he confronts the murderers fills us with admiration, even as we watch him taking their blood-smeared hands between his own. When he is left alone and turns to address his dead friend, the pent-up energy of his rage is thrilling to us: 'O pardon me, thou bleeding piece of earth/ That I am meek and gentle with these butchers!' (3.1.254). But we should not make the mistake of believing that there is anything as holy as a prophecy in the words that follow, whatever Antony may claim for them. His vision of the future is no more than a demand for revenge, a curse. Rather than offering an insight into the inevitable processes of time and nature, it deliberately calls down the horrors, the ancient and familiar horrors it anticipates. The voice of Antony, who is a true Roman, even calls for that ultimate dissociation, the indifference of mothers to their children's danger: it demands to see 'mothers...but smile when they behold/Their infants quartered with the hands of war,' (3.1.267–8).

Antony enjoys a play; he knows what he's doing when he asks to take Caesar's body out into the market place and plans to speak over it. If we yearn for the uncalculating expression of deep feeling that we can whole-heartedly subscribe to, we are not going to find that it lasts for very long in this play. The Romans seem to have disliked the way feelings change so quickly too: why else did they make such a fetish out of constancy, as if not changing were a moral virtue rather than a sign of insensibility, or unconsciousness or of death? There is one change in Antony that some editors and readers have found intolerable, so intolerable that some productions have excised it from the play. The proscription scene, as it is called, the episode that begins Act 4 and marks the dawn of the brave new world without Caesar, starts with Antony making out a list of men to be killed. One of them is the child of his own sister. Only a kind of willed blindness, a Roman blindness perhaps in the spectator, could make this action into a surprise. Shakespeare took pains to demonstrate that it was Antony's presence of mind that saw him through the dangerous moments following the murder and later prompted him to gain access to the crowd in order to play on their feelings and incite them against the party of the conspirators. But Antony wasn't just protecting himself; 'Now let it work. Mischief, thou art afoot,/Take thou what course thou wilt!' (3.2.250), he cried, as the crowd ran off carrying Caesar's body. It is the voice of a devil from the old morality plays. There is a delight in destruction for its own sake that accompanies Antony's vigour, a delight that not everyone wants to recognize as their own.

If Caesar's blindness made us wish he would get real, Antony gives us more realism than we can stomach: those decisive judgements, rather like the ones made by Goneril in *King Lear*, smack of radical contempt. 'This is a slight, unmeritable man', he dismisses Lepidus at 4.1.12. 'So is my horse', he cuts in, when Octavius objects 'But he's a tried and valiant soldier.' (4.1.28–9). Is this what Caesar, the man we have been growing almost fond of, was like in his own heyday? If so, we are increasingly adrift, with no one to look to. No wonder the Romans in this play liked the idea of Caesar as the northern star. The difficulty of holding in a single frame all the contradictory feelings that one man can inspire in us is almost overwhelming. Before the play is over we will see Antony show mercy and behave generously to a prisoner, but we will also watch as he competes with his ally Octavius almost as keenly as with those who are his foes. Yet Antony himself at the close of the play is the one who will reaffirm that hero-worship that has helped to keep all these men deaf and blind to the movement of their own inner lives.

> This was the noblest Roman of them all:
> All the conspirators, save only he,
> Did that they did in envy of great Caesar.
> He only, in a general honest thought
> And common good to all, made one of them.
>
> (5.5.68–72)

As audience, don't we know far too much to believe this, however strongly the music of the words might appeal? We at least, unlike most of the men in this play, can choose not to remain trapped inside Rome. 'A good person forced to lie suffers the guilt and self-hatred which can lead to depression and suicide', wrote psychologist Dorothy Rowe, in a comment on suicide in political life.[1] Suicide may present itself as the only way out for Romans – three of them kill themselves in the last moments of the play – but Shakespeare goes out of his way to show that another form of escape is possible. Pindarus, the man from Parthia in western Asia, who is freed by Cassius at the point of his own death, grew up in a different culture. Pindarus knows that this world of Rome is uniquely unpleasant in its surveillance and its mind-control: 'Far from this country Pindarus shall run,/Where never Roman shall take note of him', Pindarus declares (5.3.49–50). There is a space outside the mindset of Rome, Shakespeare reminds us: in a later play, *Antony and Cleopatra*, he will turn to explore that space, as he finds it outside Europe, in the land of Egypt.

Before we too leave Rome, the city which has a special place for good women, safe inside marriage, let us remember to ask what happens to the bad ones there. What happens to the women that Brutus named as harlots at 2.1? We have not been shown what makes a really bad woman in Roman terms. The play of *Julius Caesar* leaves out the story of the bad woman who was living in Rome in her own apartments across the Tiber: Cleopatra, the woman who was not Roman at all. Not until he tackled the work involved in writing *Antony and Cleopatra* would Shakespeare face the challenge of framing both Roman and Egyptian traditions side by side, to demonstrate that there was another way, a world outside the closed world of Rome, one that did not found itself on severing the connection between women and men and on worshipping pain.

At the time when Julius Caesar was put to death by his friends, at the historical moment of the events that Shakespeare's play represents, Cleopatra, the last pharaoh of Egypt, was living in Rome as Caesar's lover. She was a woman of 24. Although she was living among Romans, as Livy tells us, she insisted on being addressed by her title of queen. This may have been received as an affront to the tradition of republican Rome, but to us, who have seen two Roman wives bend the knee before their husbands on stage, it may seem proper to read

Cleopatra's demand rather differently. By what other means, let us ask ourselves, could a woman in Rome get men to treat her with equal respect? Cleopatra's rank as the independent ruler of a very rich country allowed her to refuse the subjection undergone by other women living in Rome.

If the story of Julius Caesar's relationship with Cleopatra has a tendency to wander and get lost, to keep slipping out of the frame of European history as it were, that is by no means an accident. The disappearance was engineered by Augustus, the man who in Shakespeare's play still bears his earlier name of Octavian or Octavius. The historical Octavian took the name of Augustus when he was installed as the first emperor of Rome, at the close of the twenty years of civil wars that are just getting going as Shakespeare's play comes to a close. Those wars ended with the defeat of Antony and Cleopatra at the battle of Actium. Augustus intended to punish Cleopatra, to make an example of her, as we say, so that the challenge that she mounted in her own person to the rule of Roman men and to their conception of themselves would not be repeated. It's an ambition that seems to have met with a certain success. Augustus had intended to honour the Roman tradition by leading Cleopatra in triumph through the streets of Rome. When she took her own life first, refusing to submit to such an act of violence against her spirit, Augustus had a picture of her made that was carried in his triumph instead. It was left to his court writers to name her as 'wanton' and as 'the harlot queen'. If ever we needed to be on the alert, to look out for the difference between what we are told to think and what we can see for ourselves, it is in Rome's account of Cleopatra.[2]

Caesar himself gave no evidence of wanting to humiliate Cleopatra; rather the reverse. He never publicly acknowledged the son that she bore him and named as Caesarion, it is true, but historians always concede that it was politically impossible for him to do so; 'the Senate would never have stood for it', they say. As I have been meaning to suggest, it was the formal institutions of Roman life, rather than the personal wish of individual men, that imposed such humiliation on its women. It's an institution, we say fondly sometimes, meaning that a place or a practice has resisted alteration or change. As the lover of Cleopatra, Caesar may have been moved despite himself towards a new understanding of the relation between women and men. He gave every sign of a new appreciation of tenderness that was foreign to Rome, a tenderness towards the body as a treasure of delicacy and power. In spite of the Senate and its authority, Caesar did find a way of honouring Cleopatra and making public acknowledgement of her as a mother; he had a statue of her made and covered in gold, in the form of Venus Genetrix, 'the Venus who brings forth new life', in the image, as it has been suggested, of a mother and child. Caesar made this move as a private person but his act had resonances for the state as a whole. Venus Genetrix was the tutelary deity of his own family, but she was also worshipped as the mother of the Roman people. Caesar had created a new forum, the central public space known as the Forum Julium, and built a new temple to Venus Genetrix there: that is where he set the statue of Cleopatra.

Here is the missing piece in the story of *Julius Caesar*, the piece of history that the play does not include. In that play, at the moment of crisis, when Caesar wants to know what the terrible portents mean and whether he will survive, the augurers report that 'They could not find a heart within the beast' (2.2.40). In the historical connection between Caesar and Cleopatra, have we perhaps discovered the heart that is missing from that brutalizing institution, Roman marriage? Erotic tenderness played around the figure of Cleopatra for Caesar, even while she commanded his respect.[3] Caesar recognized in Cleopatra one who was both his equal and his like.

Notes

CHAPTER 1. WHERE FANTASY AND HISTORY MEET

1   Helen Hackett, *Virgin Mother, Maiden Queen: Elizabeth I and the Cult of the Virgin Mary* (London, 1994).

CHAPTER 2. AUTHORITY AND VIOLENCE

1   Frances Baldwin, *Sumptuary Legislation and Personal Regulation in England* (Baltimore, 1926), 245.
2   Ronald C. Finucane, *Miracles and Pilgrims: Popular Beliefs in Medieval England* (London, 1977), 204.
3   The Act of Uniformity, from which I quote here, was printed as a preface to Elizabeth's Prayer Book. It has never been repealed and continues to this day, like the note on ceremonies, to be printed in the Preface to copies of the Prayer Book of the Church of England.

CHAPTER 3. WOMEN – OR STATUES?

1   Cambridge, 1989.
2   Paul Harvey (Oxford, 1937, 1980).

CHAPTER 4. PORTIA AND CALPURNIA

1   Quoted Geoffrey Miles, *Shakespeare and the Constant Romans* (Oxford, 1996), 134. n. 25.
2   Virginia Woolf, *A Room of One's Own* (London, 1929).
3   See 'Male Hysteria: W. H. R. Rivers and the Lessons of Shell-Shock', in Elaine Showalter, *The Female Malady: Women, Madness and English Culture 1830–1980* (London, 1985).

4 Estela V. Welldon, *Mother, Madonna, Whore: The Idealization and Denigration of Motherhood* (London, 1988).

5 S. Freud, 'The Infantile Genital Organisation', *Standard Edition of the Complete Psychological Works of Sigmund Freud*, vol. 19, p. 144.

6 Luce Irigaray, *This Sex Which is not One* (Ithaca, 1985).

CHAPTER 5.   WHAT CALPURNIA KNOWS

1 'Dulce et Decorum Est', *War Poems and Others*, ed. D. Hibberd (London, 1973), 79. The phrase Owen attacks is taken from Horace (*Odes*, 3.2.13).

2 *Hard Times, Oxford Illustrated Dickens*, bk. 2, ch. ix, p. 198.

3 '*Tuché* and *Automaton*', ed. Jacques-Alain Miller, trans. Alan Sheridan, in *The Four Fundamental Concepts of Psycho-Analysis* (London, 1977), 53–4.

4 'On the New Forcers of Conscience under the Long Parliament', *The Poetical Works of John Milton*, ed. Helen Darbishire (Oxford, 1955), 157.

5 New York and Oxford, 1987.

6 *Holy Feast and Holy Fast: The Religious Significance of Food to Medieval Women* (Berkeley, 1987).

7 Katharine Park personal communication. See also Lorraine Dalton and Katharine Park, *Wonders and the Order of Nature, 1150–1750* (New York, 1998).

8 André Green, *Le discours vivant* (Paris, 1973).

CHAPTER 7.   THE ESCAPE FROM DELUSION

1 'Chamber of Liars', *Guardian*, 13 August 1997.

2 For a historical analysis of Cleopatra's representation in European culture since the Renaissance, see Mary Hamer, *Signs of Cleopatra: History, Politics, Representation* (London, 1993).

3 Hamer, *Signs of Cleopatra*, 110–13.

Select Bibliography

Andrews, John F., 'Was the Bard Behind It? Old Light on the Lincoln Assassination', *Atlantic Monthly*, October 1990, pp. 26, 28, 32. Discusses the fact that the man who shot Lincoln had recently played the part of Brutus.

Barton, Anne, '*Julius Caesar* and *Coriolanus*: Shakespeare's Roman World of Words', in Philip H. Highfield Jr (ed.), *Shakespeare's Craft* (Carbondale, Ill. 1982), 24–47. Argues that in this play rhetoric is 'unequivocally poisonous'.

Belsey, Catherine, *The Subject of Tragedy: Identity and Difference in Renaissance Drama* (London, 1985). Discusses the emergence of the notion of the individual subject at the Renaissance and relates it to the simultaneous emergence of tragedy as a form.

Berry, Philippa, *Of Chastity and Power: Elizabethan Literature and the Unmarried Queen* (London, 1989, 1994). Explores the part played in the representation of power by the figure of Elizabeth's virginity.

Berry, Ralph, 'Communal Identity and the Rituals of *Julius Caesar*', in *Shakespeare and the Awareness of the Audience* (London, 1985) 75–87. Discusses the meaning of acting a part.

Bloom, Harold (ed.), *William Shakespeare's 'Julius Caesar': Modern Critical Interpretations* (New York, 1988). Anthology of essays.

Bono, Barbara, J., 'The Birth of Tragedy: Tragic Action in *Julius Caesar*', *English Literary Renaissance*, 24 (1994), 449–70. Relates to contemporary fears about transition of power at Elizabeth's approaching death.

Booth, Stephen, 'The Shakespearean Actor as Kamikaze Pilot', *Shakespeare Quarterly*, 36 (1985), 553–70. A discussion of what playing Brutus does to actors and of how they respond to criticism of their performance in the role.

Brower, Reuben, *Hero and Saint: Shakespeare and the Graeco-Roman Heroic Tradition* (Oxford, 1971). Addresses the mingling of classical and Christian in Shakespeare's works.

Charney, Maurice (ed.), *Discussions of Shakespeare's Roman Plays* (Boston, 1964). Anthology that brings together studies of the play from different periods.

Cook, Ann Jennalie, *The Privileged Playgoers of Shakespeare's London*

(Princeton, 1981). Argues in favour of a relatively well-heeled audience in the public playhouses.

Dalton, Lorraine, and Katharine Park, *Wonders and the Order of Nature, 1150–1750* (New York, 1998). Examines the way extraordinary phenomena, from miracles to curiosities, were fitted into a sense of an ordered world.

Dean, Leonard F. (ed.), *Twentieth Century Interpretations of 'Julius Caesar'* (New Jersey, 1968). Eighteen selected essays on the text.

DeGraziam, Margreta, *Shakespeare Verbatim: The Reproduction of Authenticity and the Apparatus of 1790* (Oxford, 1991). Useful account of editorial practice in the eighteenth century.

Dobson, Michael, 'Accents Yet Unknown: Canonisation and the Claiming of *Julius Caesar*', in Jean I. Marsden (ed.), *The Appropriation of Shakespeare: Post-Renaissance Reconstructions of the Works and the Myth* (Brighton, 1991). Argues that after the Restoration the play was adapted and made to seem as if it were above politics.

Drakakis, John, '"Fashion it thus": Julius Caesar and the Politics of Theatrical Representation', *Shakespeare Survey*, vol. 44, pp. 65–74. Reads the play as an unmasking of the politics of representation.

Dusinberre, Juliet, *Shakespeare and the Nature of Women* (London, 1975, 1995). The earliest full-length feminist study of Shakespeare.

Fleissner, F., 'That Philosophy in *Julius Caesar* Again', *Archiv*, 222 (1985), 344–5. An example of the unconvincing but valiant attempts to make sense of the 'philosophy' in the play.

Garber, Marjorie, *Shakespeare's Ghost Writers: Literature as Uncanny Causality* (New York and London, 1989). Discusses the way Shakespeare came to be represented as the ghost of Caesar.

Gilligan, Carol, and Lyn Mikel Brown, *Meeting at the Crossroads: Women's Psychology and Girls' Development* (Cambridge, Mass, 1992). Identifies the way girls' voices are shut down at adolescence by their education and links it with the loss of their ability to know.

Gilligan, James, *Violence: Our Deadly Epidemic* (New York, 1997). A forensic psychiatrist argues on the basis of work he has done with prisoners that violence is produced in response to the experience of humiliation.

Girard, René, *A Theatre of Envy: William Shakespeare* (Oxford, 1991). A major theorist's account of the plays: three chapters devoted to discussing the play in terms of seduction, violent polarization, and the founding murder.

Griffin, Jasper, 'Here Was a Caesar!', *New York Review of Books*, vol. 35, no. 8, p. 14. A classical scholar's assessment of the historical Caesar.

Gurr, Andrew, *Playgoing in Shakespeare's London* (Cambridge, 1987). Argues in terms of changing tastes; believes the audience was quite diverse.

Hackett, Helen, *Virgin Mother, Maiden Queen: Elizabeth I and the Cult of the Virgin Mary* (London, 1994). Historical study of Elizabeth's exploitation of religious imagery.

Hamer, Mary, *Signs of Cleopatra: History, Politics, Representation* (London, 1993). Study of the interests served in European culture at different moments by the image of Cleopatra.

―――― 'Reading *Antony and Cleopatra* Through Irigaray's *Speculum*' in *Theory and Practice: Antony and Cleopatra*, ed. N. Wood (Buckingham, 1996). Uses Irigaray as a way in to reading Shakespeare's understanding of Rome.

Hankey, Julie, 'Victorian Portias: Shakespeare's Borderline Heroine', *Shakespeare Quarterly*, vol. 45, no. 4 (winter 1994), 426-49. Discusses Portia as an example of an intellectual.

Kahn, Coppélia, *Roman Shakespeare: Warriors, Wounds and Women* (London, 1997). First feminist study of the Roman plays.

Kaula, David, '"Let us be Sacrificers": Religious Motifs in *Julius Caesar*', *Shakespeare Studies*, 14 (1981). Picks up religious elements in references to Rome but reads them in terms of English hostility to the church of Rome.

Kott, Jan, 'Caesar at the Bastille', *New York Review of Books*, 12 October 1989, 40-42. Draws attention to Buchner's appropriation of the play as 'the tragedy of history'.

Kujawinska-Courney, Krystyna, "Th'Interpretation of the Time": The Dramaturgy of Shakespeare's Roman Plays (Victoria, BC, 1993). Suggests the play asks whether Caesar should be seen as iconic or flawed.

Lutzky, Harriet, 'Reparation and *Tikkun*: A Comparison of the Kleinian and Kabbalistic Concepts', *International Review of Psychoanalysis*, 1989, vol. 16, pp. 449-57. Argues the similarity between psychoanalytic and Jewish religious models of the drive to rebuild a unity out of fragments.

―――― 'The Sacred and the Maternal Object: An Application of Fairbairn's Theory to Religion', *Psychoanalytic Reflections on Current Issues*, ed. H. Siegel *et al.* (New York, 1991). Connects object relations theory with the idea of the sacred.

Marshall, Cynthia, 'Portia's Wound; Calpurnia's Dream: Reading Character in *Julius Caesar*', *English Literary Renaissance*, 24 (1994), 471-88. Questions whether 'character' is the key to reading the action of the play.

Miles, Geoffrey, *Shakespeare and the Constant Romans* (Oxford, 1996). Reads the three plays taken from Plutarch as a triptych on the theme of Stoic constancy and manliness.

Miola, Robert S., *Shakespeare's Rome* (Cambridge, 1983). Brings together an account of Renaissance classicism with a detailed exploration of Rome's imaginative meaning for Shakespeare.

―――― 'Shakespeare and his Sources: Observations on the Critical History of *Julius Caesar*', *Shakespeare Survey*, 40 (1988), 69-77. Notes the many different ways in which Shakespeare uses Plutarch.

Mooney, Michael E., '"Passion, I See, Is Catching": The Rhetoric of *Julius Caesar*', *Journal of English and Germanic Philology*, 90 (1991), 31–50. Observes how often words denoting movement are used in scenes involving persuasion.

Parker, Barbara, L., 'The Whore of Babylon and Shakespeare's *Julius Caesar*', *Studies in English Literature*, 35 (1995), 251–70. Discusses the association of maleness and sexuality in religion.

Partridge, Loren, and Randolph Starn, *A Renaissance Likeness: Art and Culture in Raphael's Julius II* (Berkeley, 1980). Offers a detailed exploration of the way Pope Julius cultivated his public profile as a second Julius Caesar.

Pechter, Edward, '*Julius Caesar* and *Sejanus*: Roman Politics, Inner Selves and the Power of the Theatre', in E. A. J. Honigmann (ed.), *Shakespeare and his Contemporaries* (Manchester, 1986), 60–78. Discusses the value assigned to self-containment.

Rebhorn, Wayne A., 'The Crisis of the Aristocracy in *Julius Caesar*', *Renaissance Quarterly*, 43 (1990), 75–111. Detailed reading of the play as a struggle on the part of aristocrats to protect the class system.

Rose, Mark, 'Conjuring Caesar: Ceremony, History and Authority in 1599', *English Literary Renaissance*, 19 (1989), 291–304. Like Spevack's Introduction to the New Cambridge edition, this attempts to confront the irrational and its part in the play, specifically by considering popular feeling on the verge of Elizabeth's death.

Scott, William O., 'The Speculative Eye: Problematic Self-Knowledge in *Julius Caesar*', *Shakespeare Survey*, 40 (1988), 77–91. Explores failures of knowledge in the play.

Sicherman, Carol Marks, 'Short lines and Interpretation: The Case of *Julius Caesar*', *Shakespeare Quarterly*, 35 (1984), 180–95. Takes short lines in Folio text as implicit directorial hints.

Thomas, Vivian, *Julius Caesar* (Brighton, 1992). Sustained reading, including discussion of genre.

Velz, John, *Shakespeare and the Classical Tradition: A Critical Guide to Commentary 1660–1960* (Minneapolis, 1968). Annotated compilation of critical response.

Vickers, Brian, *Shakespeare: The Critical Heritage 1623–1801*, 6 vols (London, 1974). Historical compilation of critical response to each play.

Welldon, Estela V., *Mother, Madonna, Whore: The Idealization and Denigration of Motherhood* (London, 1988).

—— 'Women as Abusers', in *Planning Community Mental Health Services for Women: A Multiprofessional Handbook*, ed. K. Abel *et al.* (London, 1996), 176–89.

Wilson, Richard, *Will Power: Essays on Shakespearean Authority* (Brighton, 1993). Chapter situating the play in relation to issues of carnival and control in Shakespeare's London.

Index